STEAMING THROUGH
THE CHILTERNS
AND THEREABOUTS

GOOSE
PUBLISHING

First published in 2021

Goose Publishing, 17 Western Rd, Tring, Herts HP23 4BQ

Printed and bound in Great Britain by:

Blackmore Ltd, Longmead, Shaftesbury, Dorset, SP7 8PX.

ISBN 978-0-9543838-3-1

Photo by Bob Turnham

FOREWORD

by Robert Freeman

I, along with other local enthusiasts, was eagerly awaiting the publication of the first book, Steaming Through Berkhamsted and it was so sad that Richard Casserley didn't quite live to be there at the launch of that book. At that launch, Mary Casserley and her mother Margaret brought along some albums of Casserley photographs and other memorabilia and it was obvious that there was a great deal of potential material for at least one more book. I little dreamt that day that a sequel could still be on the cards and I would be given the honour of selecting and commenting on the photographs you will see in this book and I am extremely grateful to Mary and Margaret for allowing me access to the photographs of our local area to do this. The name Casserley is revered in Railway Circles, so it was initially quite a daunting task to do justice to the work of such icons as HCC and RMC!

I had a very tenuous link with the Casserleys in the past: another of my hobbies is philately and as a teenager, I was a member of Berkhamsted Philatelic Society which was run by HCC's wife Kathleen. She helped me enormously in shaping my collection.

For this new book, as well as revisiting the Casserley local Berkhamsted patch, I have cast the net wider to include other lines that pass through our area, The Chilterns, and a little bit further in some cases. Despite the title Steaming Through The Chilterns, I have also included some photos of early diesels and electrics as some of these had short working lives and they have also now passed into history. Photos of these are in fact rarer than those of some steam locos as many photographers of the day ignored them and gave up when steam disappeared. HCC also despised the dreaded diesel, so we are fortunate indeed that he did nonetheless take a few photos of them. As far as I am aware, many of the photographs in the book have not previously been published. However, HCC and RMC wrote so many books and contributed to so many other books and magazines, it is hard to be sure. In any case most of these are now long out of print and the photos deserve another outing. I am aware that some readers of this book will be fellow enthusiasts, but that others will be reading it out of purely local interest, so it has been difficult to know how best to pitch the captions. There may be too much detail for some and not enough for others, but as the main aim of the book is to showcase some more photos of that marvellous collection, please read or skip over the captions as you please.

ABOUT THE AUTHORS

Robert Freeman has been observing and photographing trains in his home town of Berkhamsted ever since he started trainspotting as a boy in the early 1960s. He has also travelled extensively at home and abroad in pursuit of his hobby. As a teacher at Tring School, for many years he ran a Railway Club for the students, organising regular official shed visits (when such things were still possible!), rail trips and spotting trips to the lineside all around the country. He is a member of the RCTS and is a regular at the Watford Branch and did a stint as Chairman there for a few years. He is now retired and can often be seen with his camera on Berkhamsted Station or at lineside locations nearby.

Mary Casserley grew up and went to school in Berkhamsted. Along with her three siblings, she spent many of her weekends playing in the derelict Railway Station goods-yard at the back of her granddad's house, *Ravensbourne*, in Castle Hill Close. She attended Watford School of Art followed by studying Fine Art at Portsmouth Polytechnic. She is well known for her local paintings of Berkhamsted and the Chilterns done in the style of the railway-advertising posters of the 1930s. She still lives and works in Berkhamsted with her husband and son. This is her fourth local history book, previous titles being 'Drawings of Berkhamsted High Street', 'Postcards of Berkhamsted' and 'Steaming Through Berkhamsted'. In 2017, she was elected Chairman of the Berkhamsted Local History & Museum Society.

www.marycasserley.com

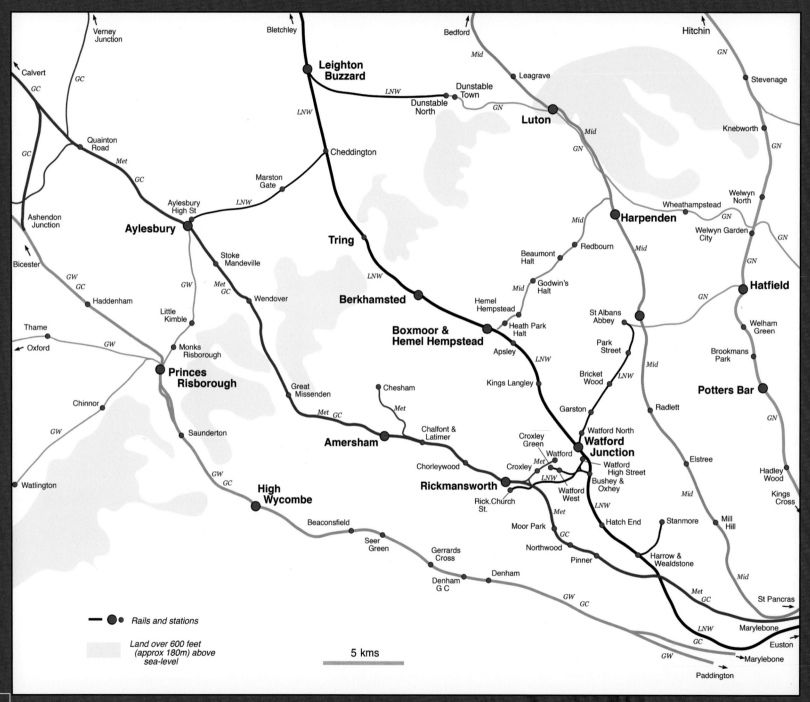

Verney Junction

Calvert

Bletchley

Bedford

Hitchin

Leighton Buzzard

Dunstable Town

Leagrave

Stevenage

Quainton Road

Cheddington

Dunstable North

Luton

Knebworth

Marston Gate

Welwyn North

Aylesbury High St

Wheathampstead

Welwyn Garden City

Ashendon Junction

Aylesbury

Stoke Mandeville

Tring

Harpenden

Beaumont Halt

Redbourn

Hatfield

Bicester

Wendover

Berkhamsted

Godwin's Halt

Little Kimble

Hemel Hempstead

Welham Green

Haddenham

Boxmoor & Hemel Hempstead

St Albans Abbey

Thame

Monks Risborough

Heath Park Halt

Park Street

Brookmans Park

Oxford

Princes Risborough

Apsley

Bricket Wood

Potters Bar

Chinnor

Great Missenden

Kings Langley

Chesham

Garston

Radlett

Saunderton

Watlington

Amersham

Chalfont & Latimer

Watford North

Watford Junction

Elstree

Chorleywood

Croxley Green

Hadley Wood

High Wycombe

Rickmansworth

Croxley

Watford

Watford High Street

Kings Cross

Rick. Church St.

Watford West

Bushey & Oxhey

Mill Hill

Beaconsfield

Moor Park

Hatch End

Stanmore

Seer Green

Northwood

Gerrards Cross

Pinner

Harrow & Wealdstone

St Pancras

Denham G C

Denham

Marylebone

Euston

Marylebone

Paddington

Rails and stations

Land over 600 feet (approx 180m) above sea-level

5 kms

GC, Met, LNW, GW, GN, Mid

4

CHILTERNS

We have used the regional name Chilterns since these hills are the edge of the huge geological saucer with London at its centre. We have strayed a little beyond into the Aylesbury Vale to the Northwest and to the Southeast to include Amersham, Rickmansworth, Watford, St Albans, Hatfield and Potters Bar where the Chilterns geological structure lies deeper, but are on the climb towards the Chiltern summits from the London termini.

The first line to tackle this barrier to rail-progress was the LNWR towards the Berkhamsted/Tring gap. It arrived at Boxmoor in the mid-1830s and was thwarted in its hope of crossing the Chilterns by the most obvious gap, the Hemel Hempstead route, by local land-owner opposition, and was forced to come via Berkhamsted which necessitated the Northchurch tunnel and then the monstrous Tring cutting.

HCC chose his home near the summit of this route and many of his photos are of the locos in their final rush, working hard, towards the top of the gradient, over a hundred metres higher than Euston, or coasting down to the London terminus.

INTRODUCTION

by Chris Green - ex MD Network SouthEast: MD InterCity & CEO Virgin Trains

What an inspired idea to publish a sequel to the late Henry Casserley's iconic photographic collection 'Steaming through Berkhamsted'!

I suspect that the idea was born at the launch of the original book, as I well remember the look of awe on Rob Freeman's face when he was allowed to inspect the albums from the family collection - and I cannot think of a more qualified person to help Mary Casserley mine the rich seam of railway history from her grandfather's priceless albums.

I am delighted that Rob Freeman has put his talents to such good use as I am very aware that he and H.C. Casserley share very similar skills and interests. They are both highly regarded railway photographers who have lived in Berkhamsted for much of their lives: they are both big names in the Railway Correspondence & Travel Society, where HCC used to organise rail tours and Rob is an active member in our local Watford Branch - and they are both highly respected for their knowledge of railway history and traction.

The result is a second book filled with new railway scenes which have never been published before and which provide a fascinating view of railway activities in the Home Counties ranging from the Second World War to the Beeching '60s. Rob Freeman has used his scholarship to write and research definitive captions for each photograph which add an extra dimension to the book.

There is something for everyone in a book that takes us back to post-war Britain in the Home Counties. Social history merges with railway history as the record moves from an immaculate Royal Train passing Potters Bar in 1938 to the appalling winter scenes of 1947, the electrification of mainlines and the slow death of nostalgic rural branches.

So do enjoy this unique and well researched book!

Berkhamsted

Over the years HCC took many hundreds of photos in his local area around Berkhamsted. Inevitably there was room for only a small proportion of them in the first book and many excellent photos had to be omitted. Here then, to start this new book, is a further selection of a few more taken between Bourne End and Northchurch, serving as a quick recap of what the first book was all about.

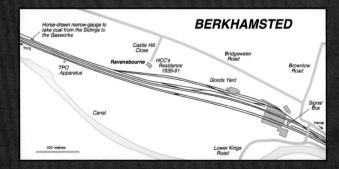

Firstly we see a northbound local train nearing Bourne End with Hemel Hempstead and Boxmoor station (as it was then named) in the distance on 19th August 1939. The locomotive is "Crab" 2-6-0 **2817**. On page 121 of the first book there is a photo of another of this class on a local train at Northchurch tunnel and Richard Casserley remarked that these locos were somewhat unusual for this type of working: indeed only a small proportion of the 245-strong class were allocated down south, though they often worked in from the north on freight trains. Richard also caused a bit of head scratching amongst enthusiasts by referring to the class as "Spiders", a nickname we had never heard before, but apparently it was used by HCC's generation.

This particular example was a local Willesden engine until January 1951 when it moved on to Nuneaton, then Aston and finally Stockport from where it was withdrawn in April 1965.

The "and Boxmoor" was dropped from the station name on 20 December 1963. However the station really is at Boxmoor (the original name for the station) and is some distance from Hemel Hempstead town centre, even more so from the original Hemel Hempstead Old Town. The train is passing the site of where new high speed crossovers were installed in the early 2000s as part of the West Coast main line upgrade.

On the same day, 19th August 1939, HCC has now moved a bit further north and is standing in Bourne End signal box to take this photo of a northbound express. It is headed by Patriot Class (or "Baby Scot") **5545 *Planet***. 18 of this 52-strong class were later rebuilt with larger taper boilers and this was one of them, being converted in November 1948. It then served at a variety of West Coast main sheds until May 1964 when it was withdrawn from Carlisle Upperby.

The train is passing the crossovers at Bourne End which were the site of the terrible accident in 1945 which was described and illustrated in the first book. The speed limit was 15-20 mph for such crossovers and to save construction costs they surprisingly lived on into the high speed electric age (though not these ones) until the major upgrade of the line in the early 2000s.

Of the hundreds of photos HCC took here, relatively few were at Berkhamsted station itself and even fewer south of the station: he seems to have preferred his "patch" from his house *Ravensbourne* northwards to Northchurch Tunnel. However here are a couple of beauties taken on 24th February 1947, during one of the worst winters of the 20th century.

Below left: Jubilee Class 4-6-0 **5721 *Impregnable*** storms through on the down fast with a northbound express, leaving a magnificent steamy exhaust in the cold air. This loco served at a variety of West Coast sheds in its career which ended at Bank Hall (Liverpool) in October 1965.

Below right: Another Jubilee, **5683 *Hogue***, is coming the other way past the signal box with an up express. Note also the headshunt between the fast and slow lines and on Platform 1 is one of the original lifts, which was for parcels traffic, not for passengers.

Soon ***Hogue*** would be a rare visitor here as it spent its entire career based at Millhouses (Sheffield). It was withdrawn in the mass cull of steam locos in December 1962. We shall return to some more snow scenes in a later chapter.

On 14th April 1953 Fowler 2-6-4T **42304** is arriving into Platform 4 with the 7.32am Tring-Euston. Six months previously this had been the service involved in the tragic Harrow and Wealdstone disaster. HCC usually travelled on this train in the rear carriage and had he not been off work with bronchitis that fateful day, he would have become another victim. 42304 was a local IC Watford engine, but it moved north to Uttoxeter just two months later and then on to Longsight in Manchester. It came back to Willesden in 1958-9 before going all the way north to Carlisle Kingmoor from where it was withdrawn in September 1962.

On the right in the photo is the Casserley home *Ravensbourne* which HCC had had built specially in 1938. The goods yard is well stocked with wagons and some of the splendid semaphore signals are in view. They had to be tall to improve sighting on the sweeping S-bend through the station. The down slow starter signal is a distinctive feature, being adapted from a LNWR bracket. In recent times the platforms have been lengthened to take 12-car trains and extend to roughly where the second coach in this train is. The goods yard, as at so many stations, is now the site of the station car park and Ravensbourne is now only visible in the winter as the trees have grown up so much.

From the angle of the sun this is an evening commuter train from Euston hauled by Black Five 4-6-0 **44874** on 4th August 1949. HCC's diary records that he took young Richard to Cheddington that evening to "cop" 0-6-2 Webb Coal Tank **46666** on the Aylesbury branch line train. It is hard to imagine now, but at this time, and until electrification in the 1960s, the local passenger service was a very sparse one and there were less services per day than there are in less than a couple of hours nowadays!

44874 was based at Bletchley at the time and moved on to Crewe in January 1950. It then served at various sheds in the North West, finally at Carnforth, and lasted till the very end of steam in August 1968.

It's "only a Black Five" as we used to say (well there were 842 of them!), but this one is clean and putting on a fine display as it heads a northbound express on 2nd May 1953. **44737** was based at Blackpool at the time, so this might be a clue as to the destination of the train. It stayed at Blackpool until September 1964 when it moved on to Bolton, Liverpool and finally Wigan, from where it was withdrawn in January 1967.

Here, just north of Berkhamsted station Platform 1, was one of HCC's favourite spots for taking photos.

Royal Scot 4-6-0 **46115 *Scots Guardsman*** is passing platform 1 with the down Shamrock (Euston-Liverpool) on 23rd July 1955. Berkhamsted is 28 miles by rail from London Euston and milepost 28 can be seen just off the end of the platform. Scots Guardsman was a long term resident of Longsight (Manchester) shed from 1949 until September 1960 when it started to move around various North-West sheds, ending up at Carlisle Kingmoor from where it was withdrawn in December 1965. It was one of two of the class (the other being 46100 Royal Scot itself) lucky to escape the cutter's torch and after a lengthy period out of service is now restored for main line running, mainly in the North-West, again like Royal Scot. However both these engines have once again passed through Berkhamsted a couple of times in recent years. As we shall see in a later chapter, HCC had spent this day on the Met and GC line to Aylesbury and obviously stopped to photograph this train on his way home.

On 8th June 1945 Princess Coronation streamlined Pacific **Queen Mary** heads a northbound express into the evening sunshine. The loco is wearing a thick coating of wartime grime (note that it has been cleaned only around the number **6222**) and without the handsome lining out it really does look a bit of an ugly bulbous beast! The casing was removed from the class and the last one (46243) was done in 1949.

As BR 46222 this loco has a fond memory for me. For the whole of its BR career it was a Polmadie (Glasgow) locomotive. Steam locos need more frequent servicing than modern traction, so on long journeys there would be engine changes. This meant that the Polmadie engines were difficult to see at the southern end of the WCML. I had just started trainspotting and in summer 1962 I was with some fellow spotters down by the canal by the Crystal Palace pub just south of the station (where we also liked to watch the coal barges go past on the canal). 46222 appeared and one of the older members of the group started whooping with joy. I didn't understand why at the time, being a novice at the hobby and not understanding the subtleties of locomotive allocations! I still have the notebook from that summer (see inset) and in fact 46222 appears twice in it. The loco was withdrawn in October 1963, a year before all the survivors (about half of the class of 38) were suddenly withdrawn en masse.

Below: A lovely sunny evening view of a northbound local train in LMS days before the war. With a fine array of private-owner wagons in the yard in the foreground, LMS Compound 4-4-0 **1153** accelerates away from the station stop on 29th May 1939. This class was a development of the Midland Railway design and was a particular favourite of the Casserleys. This particular example lasted until November 1957 when it was withdrawn from Bourneville, though it had spent most of its BR career based at Chester.

Here are two shots taken from the area now called Canal Fields, just north of Berkhamsted Station.

Firstly, we have a low angle view of Patriot 4-6-0 **45528 R.E.M.E.** (though it was to be another ten years before it was so named) working hard on a northbound express on Sunday 30th October 1949. It was one of 18 of the class of 52 locomotives to be rebuilt with a taper boiler and was yet to be fitted with smoke deflectors. Allocated to Crewe at this time, it was to move around the principal sheds of the WCML, spending its last couple of years based locally at Willesden before withdrawal in January 1963.

Secondly, on Sunday 10th October 1948, Black Five 4-6-0 **4811** is piloting Royal Scot 4-6-0 **46122 Royal Ulster Rifleman** on another down express. As this was a Sunday, the train is running on the slow line, probably because of engineering work. They are passing over an occupation bridge which nowadays is a footpath underpass from the residential roads behind leading to the "Blue Bridge" over the canal. There was no need for such a bridge back then as the houses were yet to be built and there were only green fields behind.

It is early BR days and 4811 is still in LMS livery, based at Saltley in Birmingham at the time. It spent its life at sheds in the Midlands and was withdrawn from Annesley in October 1966. 46122 is carrying its new BR number, but is otherwise still in LMS guise. It was to be a long-term resident of Longsight in Manchester at the time and then moved around a bit at the end of its career and was one of the class to end up on the former

Great Central, also based at Annesley. In October 1964 it was reallocated to Carlisle, but as it was withdrawn the same month, it was probably too rundown to actually work from there!

HCC's newly built house *Ravensbourne* stands out in the background as another Black 5 4-6-0 **5330** passes with a down express on 10th July 1939. It is passing under the outer home signal gantry that controlled trains to proceed to the next section on to Tring on the down slow and fast lines.

This was a long-lived member of the class which moved around the North West and even had a short spell in Scotland in 1951. It spent 11 years at Carlisle Kingmoor and ended up at Carnforth for the very end of steam in August 1968.

Watched by a young Richard Casserley in his Berkhamsted School uniform, cap and raincoat, an express storms through just north of the station, passing the TPO apparatus, on 9th September 1946. It is double-headed by a Black 5 4-6-0 **5296** and an as yet un-rebuilt Royal Scot 4-6-0 **6140 *The King's Royal Rifle Corps.***

As BR 45296 this Black 5 spent many years at Carlisle Upperby until 1963 when it moved south to Patricroft (Manchester), then Wigan and lasted into the last year of steam, being withdrawn from Liverpool Edge Hill in February 1968.

6140 was one of the last ten of the class to be rebuilt, not being so treated until 1952. As 46140 it was a local Camden loco until 1950, then it moved around various London Midland region sheds. In 1959 it spent three months based on the Midland Main Line, then moved to Carlisle Kingmoor from where it was withdrawn as one of the last survivors in October 1965. This is another loco which I myself remember well: one day in around 1962-3

I was walking home from school (dressed very much the same as RMC in the photo!) and it drifted through heading north in absolutely sparkling ex-works condition. It must therefore have been one of the last to have a major overhaul which would explain it being one of the last ones to go.

A powerful picture of Princess Coronation Pacific **46233 *Duchess of Sutherland*** storming north with the down Merseyside Express in the evening of 9th August 1963. It is passing the Travelling Post Office pick-up apparatus that featured in the first book. 46233 is likely to have been substituting for a failed diesel as by this date all the principal expresses were in the hands of the English Electric Type 4s (later Class 40s).

46233 was a Liverpool Edge Hill loco at the time, so was heading home. It lasted there until February 1964. However it was to become one of the three lucky ones to be preserved. Initially it went on display at Butlins Heads-of-Ayr holiday camp and then moved to Bressingham Steam Museum. In 1996 it was purchased by the Princess Royal Class Locomotive Trust at Butterley where it was restored to main line running condition which was completed in 2001. In effect it took over being the main line flagship from 46229 Duchess of Hamilton which had retired to be re-streamlined and put on static display at the National Railway Museum in York. On its travels back on the main line it has once again passed through Berkhamsted several times.

One of those lucky shots photographers dream of getting! Fowler 2-6-4T **42303** on a down local is being overtaken by a down express hauled by Royal Scot 4-6-0 **46169 _The Boy Scout_** about half a mile north of Berkhamsted station on New Year's Day 1949. The field on the left is now occupied by housing.

42303 was a Bletchley engine at the time, but a couple of years later it started to move around the London Midland Region, being withdrawn from Wigan in October 1962. 46169 was a long term resident of Longsight (Manchester), staying there until July 1959 when it moved to Crewe. In April 1962 it came south to Willesden, and from there in January 1963 it moved to the former Great Central at Annesley. Like others of the class that were allocated there at the time, it was by then in a very run-down condition and only lasted in service there for a few months, being withdrawn in May 1963.

The Fowler 2P 4-4-0s were not particularly common on the southern part of the West Coast Main Line, but this one No. **672** (later 40672) spent its entire career at Watford shed (1C) until it was withdrawn in October 1962. It was allocated to the District Engineer and his Inspection Saloon, but when not needed, it could be found on other local duties, as seen here. With what appears to be a train of ballast for track maintenance, 672 is passing *Ravensbourne* just north of the station in the evening sun on 15th September 1946.

This is another photo of a loco which featured in the first book. It features what was to be the very last of the Claughton Class 4-6-0s, **6004** on a down goods on 9th June 1939. It looks as if the driver is playing to the camera and the train could be restarting after a signal check. There were a couple of other survivors of the class at this date, but they had all gone by 1941 leaving 6004 to soldier on alone until April 1949, based at Liverpool Edge Hill. It never received the allocated BR number 46004. *Ravensbourne*, which stands out so prominently in the background, is nowadays dwarfed by other housing and trees.

It is 23rd August 1958 and by this date LMS Compound 4-4-0s were becoming rare. However judging by the Casserley photos, this was a last regular working for them, the 3.05 Saturdays only Euston-Rugby. Here **41167** has just passed under Billet Lane, Northchurch, with this train. Where the gasworks stood so prominently there is now an industrial estate and housing has replaced the green fields on the other side of the line.41167 had come to Rugby shed the previous May, but would only last there for another two months before being withdrawn in October.

From the other side of the line and a little further north we see Stanier 8F 2-8-0 **8042** on down empties returning to the Midlands coal fields on 7th June 1939, passing some interestingly placed distant signals for Berkhamsted. This was another of Stanier's masterpiece workhorses, some of which, like his Black 5s, lasted till the very end of steam. It was one of the designs that the War Department adopted and had built for war service. They also requisitioned 51 LMS built examples and this loco was one of those. It was sent to the Middle East and, like many others, sadly did not return, so it never became BR 48042. As a young trainspotter, it took me a while to realise why there were so many gaps in the 8Fs in the spotting book!

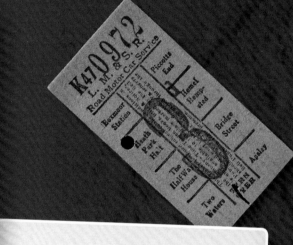

Two views on a glorious sunny evening on the 18th May 1948 of up trains at the southern exit from Northchurch tunnel. As it is just five months into Nationalisation, both locos are still in LMS livery. *Right:* 4F 0-6-0 **(4)4046** with an up goods: just look at all those tarpaulins! The loco was a visitor from Burton where it was based until May of the following year when it moved to Rowsley for the rest of its career which ended in August 1963.

Black 5 4-6-0 **(4)4768** drifts out of the tunnel with an up special working. This was a Crewe North loco at the time, but then in April 1950 it moved to Liverpool Edge Hill where it stayed until it was withdrawn in May 1967.

We now move to the north end of the tunnel. On the glorious summer evening of 11th August 1939, Princess Royal Pacific **6201 *Princess Elizabeth*** heads the down Merseyside Express, the 6.05pm from Euston to Liverpool. The loco was built in 1933 and was named after our Queen when she was a young girl. It was withdrawn as 46201 in October 1962. We see it here during the only two months in its career when it was allocated to Longsight. Otherwise at various times it was allocated to Camden, Crewe, Edge Hill and Polmadie, ending up in Carlisle. That was not the end of the story as it lingered for a time in store at Carlisle along with 46200. It was then the one of the pair to enter preservation, initially at Ashchurch in Gloucestershire, then at the Bulmers Railway Centre in Hereford and then at Butterley. It has been a frequent main line runner over the years, but has also had to undergo lengthy periods out of service for overhaul and maintenance at various preservation workshops. It was one of the first steam locomotives to work on our section of line in the preservation era and elsewhere it has even worked the Royal Train.

Jubilee Class 4-6-0 **5723** *Fearless* heads a northbound fitted goods out of Northchurch tunnel on the evening of 6th June 1939. The continuous vacuum brakes of fitted goods meant that these trains could travel faster than the plodding 20mph or so of the then more common goods trains made up of unbraked wagons which relied on the braking power of the locomotive and brakevan at the rear. This explains why we see a more normally express passenger loco on this working.

The two single bores of the slow lines were added when the line was quadrupled in 1875. As can be seen, there was already some housing above the north side of the tunnel back then, but nowadays it is built up with residential roads from over the top of the tunnel all the way back to Berkhamsted Station.

Fearless served at various times based at Longsight (for a long period), Crewe, Carlisle and Rugby, finishing up at Nuneaton from where it was withdrawn in August 1964.

Lines Around Princes Risborough

Leaving the West Coast Main Line for the moment, we will now take a look at some other lines in our area, moving from west to east, starting at Princes Risborough.

In steam days Princes Risborough, on the Great Central and Great Western Joint Line, was a fascinating place for the Railway Enthusiast. What had started out as a station on the Aylesbury and Maidenhead branch line had grown into a major junction with two platforms, each with a bay at the north end and through running lines in the middle: there was a large goods yard as well. Looking north, in clockwise order, were the branch to Chinnor and Watlington, the cross country through branch to Thame and Oxford (a useful diversionary route), the Great Western main line to Birmingham Snow Hill and Wolverhampton Low level, dividing off that a few miles to the north at Ashendon Junction was the Great Central link to their main line at Grendon Underwood Junction and finally the original branch to Aylesbury We will have a look at each of these. From the south trains would arrive on the Joint Line from either the Marylebone or Paddington directions (the routes joined at Northolt Junction).

Passenger services on the Watlington branch were the first to go, in 1957, but the line remained open for freight to Chinnor Cement Works until 1989. Passenger services to Thame went in 1963, but again the line remained open for freight traffic to an oil terminal at Thame which finished in 1991. The Great Central Main Line closed in September 1966, though the link through Ashendon and Grendon Underwood had already seen decreasing use since 1960. After an Indian Summer in the early 1960s, when more Birmingham trains ran while the West Coast Main Line was being electrified, the Great Western Main Line was then singled and became a backwater local line to Banbury. This created one of the longest stretches of single line without a passing loop in the country, that between Princes Risborough and Bicester and this severely limited the capacity of the service. Remarkably the branch to Aylesbury was retained, principally as it provided a very useful alternative through route to Marylebone.

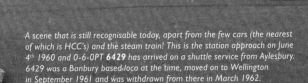

*A scene that is still recognisable today, apart from the few cars (the nearest of which is HCC's) and the steam train! This is the station approach on June 4th 1960 and 0-6-0PT **6429** has arrived on a shuttle service from Aylesbury. 6429 was a Banbury based loco at the time, moved on to Wellington in September 1961 and was withdrawn from there in March 1962.*

So by the early 1980s, Princes Risborough was in a sorry run-down state. The down platforms had been closed and their buildings demolished and the footbridge was falling into disrepair. Trains in both directions had to call at the same platform, again limiting the service. On the plus side, the Aylesbury bay was retained as were the original station buildings. There was talk of Marylebone closing and the line out of it was to be converted into a bus way. Fortunately nothing came of that nonsense and today the line has enjoyed a complete turnround in fortune under Chiltern Railways. The down platform has been reinstated and a new footbridge built. Main line services once again run through to Birmingham (and on to Kidderminster), but from Marylebone rather than Paddington. There are also trains once more to Oxford, not via Thame, but via a new connection put in at Bicester. Freight trains containing spoil and refuse from London share the Aylesbury branch with passenger trains to reach Calvert for dumping in the old brick clay pits. Even better news came in 2019 when The Chinnor and Princes Risborough Railway achieved its goal of reaching a re-opened platform 4, so steam trains once again serve the station. The occasional main line steam train also passes through, though not nearly as many as in the late 1980s when there were frequent steam specials to Stratford-Upon-Avon on Sundays.

*A closer view over the fence from the approach road of another Aylesbury shuttle train with 0-4-2T **1473** about to propel the 11.15 service formed of Hawksworth auto trailer W225W on 23rd July 1955. This bay is still used today for Aylesbury trains, though the run-round loop on the right is long gone. 1473 was then locally based at Aylesbury. It moved to Gloucester in January 1961 and was withdrawn from there in August 1962. The auto trailer was built as late as 1951 and is now preserved on the South Devon Railway.*

HCC was obviously enjoying the action in the morning sunshine that day, 23rd July 1955, as a bit later on from the previous photo 0-4-2T **1473** is arriving back from Aylesbury with the 12.05 service from there. Also approaching is another auto trailer service, the 11.36 from Bicester, hauled by 0-6-0 Pannier Tank **5409**. All the intermediate stations it had served are now long closed, the present Haddenham and Thame Parkway station being on a different site from the original

Haddenham Station. On the left is the magnificent signal box, one of the largest on the former GWR system. Fortunately, though redundant, it survived the modern re-signalling of the line and has been preserved and can occasionally be visited by arrangement on Open Days.

5409 was a local Aylesbury loco and remained so until it was withdrawn in June 1959.

Hall Class 4-6-0 **5900 *Hinderton Hall*** storms through on the middle road at Princes Risborough with the 10.10 from Birmingham Snow Hill to Ramsgate holiday express on Saturday 23rd July 1955, Such a display of dirty smoke was not typical of a Great Western locomotive and would have been frowned upon in some circles!

On the left, part of a coach of the Watlington Branch train can be glimpsed in the down bay platform. The Aylesbury bay is on the right and semaphore signals abound.

5900 was a Tyseley based loco at the time and was withdrawn in December 1963 from Bristol St Philips Marsh. This was one of the lucky members of the class which entered preservation via being rescued from Woodham's scrapyard in Barry. It has always been based at the Didcot Railway Centre and was one of the first to be restored to working order in the 1970s and ran for a time on the main line.

The Great Central route brought LNER locos to the area, greatly adding to the variety of trains to see. Here B1 Class 4-6-0 **1109** brings through a long southbound goods formed of wooden-bodied wagons on 26th July 1947 past the signal box and a fine array of semaphore signals.

As BR 61109 this locomotive spent the 1950s allocated to Stratford. It was one of the locomotives loaned to the Southern Region in May 1953 to cover for the Merchant Navy Pacifics which had temporarily been withdrawn for inspection following the failure of a centre driving wheel axle at speed on one of the class, 35020 Bibby Line, at Crewkerne. Later, when displaced by the dieselisation of East Anglia, 61109 moved north to the Sheffield area in December 1960 and was withdrawn from Peterborough New England in July 1964.

The date is given as 26th May 1962, but it must've nonetheless been a very chilly day, judging by the amount of steam escaping from the locomotive and the train heating of the carriage and yet it is early afternoon. We are looking across to the down platform at 2-6-2 Prairie Tank **5101** waiting to leave with the 2.30pm to Banbury. 5101 was the class leader of this variant of 2-6-2 tanks, a type much favoured by the GWR for branch line and suburban work. It had been a long-term resident of Stourbridge Shed until it moved to Leamington Spa in June 1957 from where it would be withdrawn in June 1963.

The coach is auto trailer **W220W** *Thrush*. Such vehicles were designed for lightweight branch or country local services and could either be hauled conventionally or pushed by a specially fitted locomotive with the driver controlling it from the front of the coach, thus reducing the need for shunting manoeuvres. The fireman had to stay on the locomotive to carry out his duties of course. However, this particular type of locomotive was not fitted for this kind of working, so would have had to run round its train at the end of each journey.

Looking north from the footbridge on 19th July 1952 we see King Class 4-6-0 **6016 *King Edward V*** rushing through on the middle road with the 8.55 from Birkenhead to Paddington. The thirty engines of this class were the ultimate in Great Western steam power and were the most powerful 4-6-0s in the country. Because of their weight they were restricted to the main lines. Just like its classmates, 6016 spent time moving around between the sheds Old Oak Common, Stafford Road (Wolverhampton) and Laira (Plymouth). The whole class suddenly went in 1962 with the onset of dieselisation.

Fortunately three of them are preserved. 6000 *King George V* is currently on display at the STEAM museum in Swindon. 6023 *King Edward II* is at Didcot, currently in working order (though its boiler certificate ran out in 2020) and is in early British Railways blue livery. 6024 *King Edward I*, which was originally restored locally at Quainton Road in 1989, is undergoing restoration on the West Somerset Railway. Both 6000 and 6024 have worked on the main line in preservation: indeed in 1971 6000 led the way to main line preserved steam running by being the first to break the steam ban imposed by BR in 1968.

0-6-0PT **3608** brings a mixed goods train off the Thame line on Saturday 23rd July 1955. This design of locomotive was unique to the Great Western and many hundreds of them were built. 3608 was an Oxford loco at the time and still had ten years' service in front of it. In 1958 it moved to the London area, serving at Slough, Old Oak Common and finally Southall from where it was withdrawn in June 1965, the last year of former Great Western steam power. The building visible on the left is part of the Forest Products Research Laboratory which was set up there in 1927 and served until it closed in 1988. In its day it carried out all kinds of research into issues to do with timber products, including such problems as Deathwatch beetle, dry rot and Dutch elm disease.

Here is another goods train coming from the Great Central line on 1st November 1958. The locomotive is Gresley V2 2-6-2 **60915**, arguably one of the most handsome designs of steam locomotive ever produced, one of "the engines that won the war". 184 of them were built and they could turn their hand to almost any kind of traffic and could match the more famous LNER Pacifics in performance. 60915 was based at the time at Woodford Halse, the heart of the former GC system. When the former GC route was transferred from the Eastern to the London Midland Region, 60915 moved to the North-east and was withdrawn from Darlington in November 1962.

Note that the signals were a mixture of upper and lower quadrants.

What a marvellous portrait of a Great Western railmotor train! Such trains could be seen on branch lines all over the GW system, but this one has worked a local service on the main line and 0-4-2T **1426** has recently arrived with the 4.40 train from Banbury on 26th July 1947, see below. It is now in the middle of its shunting manoeuvres across the lines to work its train back and it is seen here on the down through road. 1426 was a local Aylesbury based loco at the time but from 1951 onwards it started to roam all over the former GW system, finally being withdrawn from Gloucester in April 1962. The auto trailer coach is W81W which was built in 1912 and lasted in service until March 1958.

Thompson L1 2-6-4T **67778** engaged in a bit of shunting on the west side of the station is seen from the down bay platform, again on 23rd July 1955. The rebuilt platform for the Chinnor and Princes Risborough Railway is here and now no longer has a buffer stop, but extends through the platform to some sidings and to join the line 67778 is standing on, which forms a run-round loop.

The prototype L1 was built in 1945, but the main build of 99 more locos wasn't constructed until British Railways days, in 1948-50. They weren't particularly successful as they were intended for fast suburban passenger work, but were in fact more suited to low speed branch freight work. Consequently the suburban work caused parts to wear out rather too quickly. Before the problems could be fully sorted out, the class was overtaken by the introduction of Multiple Units and all were withdrawn between 1960 and 1962. 67778 was a local engine based at Neasden but spent its last 17 months at New England, Peterborough, from where it was withdrawn in May 1962.

The Watlington branch train waits in the down bay platform on 23rd July 1955 headed by another GWR 0-6-0PT **9722** which was a long term resident of Slough shed until it was withdrawn in July 1962. The coach is W85W a Churchward auto trailer which was already 43 years old at the time of this photo and which had another two years to go in service. 9722 was not auto-fitted and would have to run round at Watlington.

We are now at the other end of the branch, at Watlington itself, and 0-6-0 pannier tank **4638** has just arrived with the 1.54 from Princes Risborough on 19th July 1952. There are many typical features of a GWR branch line: gas lamps, "parachute" water tower, signal cabin and a not so typical ramshackle carriage shed.

4638 had only just been transferred south to Slough from Stourbridge two months previously. It then stayed a local engine for the rest of its career, at Slough, until 1963 when it moved on to Old Oak Common and then Southall from where it was withdrawn in June 1965, just six months from the end of Western Region steam.

After the line closed to passengers in 1957, goods traffic continued until 1960 when the line closed south of Chinnor. Traffic continued to the cement works at Chinnor until 1989. Back on the 14th October 1957 the daily goods is passing Lewknor Bridge Halt, the last station before Watlington. In July 1957 two former LNER J15 0-6-0s, 65390 and 65405 were transferred from East Anglia to Neasden, so instead of the usual former Great Western steam power seen on the line, **65390** was doing the honours that day. The two locos didn't last long in the area and were withdrawn in 1958.

A little later the same loco is seen passing Aston Rowant on the return trip. It appears that there was no load that day on this section of the line.

Two views of Chinnor station on 13th September 1958, looking towards Princes Risborough (above) and towards Watlington (below). These views will look familiar to anyone who has visited the current Chinnor and Princes Risborough Railway, but all the buildings in these photos were later demolished and those we see today have been carefully reconstructed by the Preservationists.

Back at Watlington, we see a strengthened train waiting to head back to Princes Risborough. There are quite a few people milling about, but this is no happy occasion as it is the last day that passenger services ran, Saturday 29th June 1957. The train is the 7.15 pm departure headed by 0-6-0 pannier tank **4650** of Slough shed. In May 1960 this loco would be transferred away to Wales and lasted to the last year of Western Region steam, being withdrawn in July 1965.

With a train full of passengers taking a last ride on the branch, 4650 chuffs off into history in a cloud of steam.

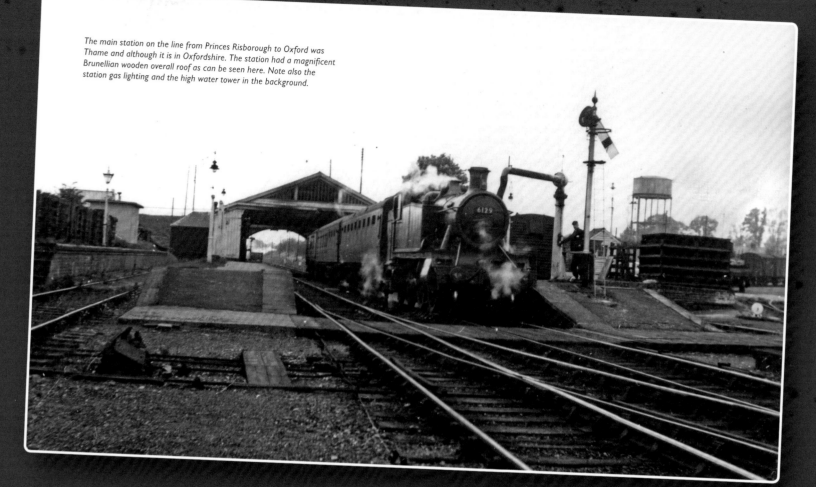

The main station on the line from Princes Risborough to Oxford was Thame and although it is in Oxfordshire. The station had a magnificent Brunellian wooden overall roof as can be seen here. Note also the station gas lighting and the high water tower in the background.

On 26th May 1962, 2-6-2 Prairie tank **6129** is heading an Oxford to Princes Risborough train and is taking water during the station stop. This version of the 2-6-2 tank was constructed mainly for hauling suburban trains in the London area, but in BR days some moved elsewhere as they became displaced by DMUs.

Princes Risborough to Oxford trains were withdrawn in 1963, though freight trains continued from Risborough to serve a BP oil depot just west of this station until 1991.

The Oxford end of the line is still open for freight as far as Morris Cowley and has been busy with car trains. There has even been talk of reopening this section to passengers.

6129 was based at Oxford, so a regular on the line at the time. Three months later it was transferred to Banbury and then spent its final nine months in service at Stourbridge, being withdrawn in September 1965, almost at the end of Western Region steam.

We now switch to the branch line that is still open today, that between Princes Risborough and Aylesbury, which was originally part of the Maidenhead and Aylesbury Railway. The first station out from Princes Risborough was the halt at Monks Risborough which was opened as late as 11th November 1929. In the 1920s and 30s the GWR opened up many halts on its branches to try and boost traffic in the face of increasing road competition. It was common for GWR branch trains to be formed of a locomotive sandwiched between auto trailers, though in this case the trailing coach appears to be a parcels van.

On 4th June 1960 **6429** has just left the halt heading for Aylesbury. We have already seen this train in the station approach road scene at Princes Risborough. HCC was to be congratulated for keeping his car in immaculate ex-works condition!

We are still at Monks Risborough, on the platform this time and 0-6-0 pannier tank **6403** is approaching the halt with the 1.25pm from Aylesbury with Collett Brake Third coach number W5617W built in 1931, which had less than a year left in service.

6403 was a Banbury based loco and later moved to Wellington and Stourbridge and was withdrawn in December 1963.

36

A neat and tidy Little Kimble station on 8th July 1939 looking towards Aylesbury. The station is still open today, but the building has been sold off, then enlarged and is now a private house. There is not even this meagre canopy shelter for today's passengers.

HCC notes in his diary that this was taken during a Saturday family day out and that he bought two gallons of petrol in Stoke Mandeville for 3/6d, that's 17 and a half pence in today's money! However in real terms of purchasing power that equates to over £11 today, so in fact petrol was more expensive then.

On 1st November 1958 prairie tank **6154** is approaching bunker-first with the 3.20pm Aylesbury to Paddington. 6154 was a Slough loco until 1960 when it moved a bit down the line to Oxford for its last five years in traffic.

Today, as then, the service consists of a mixture of shuttles and through services. In 2017 enthusiasts flocked to the line, as the rush hour shuttles were being worked by two Class 121 single car DMUs, affectionately known as Bubble Cars. These were the very last of the first generation DMU vehicles (which dated back to the late 1950s and early 1960s) to remain in traffic on Network Rail and they finished work on May 19th 2017. Fortunately they entered preservation, but not locally: the Chinnor and Princes Risborough Railway does have two others of the class though.

ASHENDON JUNCTION

The Great Central Railway opened its London Extension in 1899 using the Metropolitan Railway tracks via Aylesbury to gain access to London. However this caused capacity problems, particularly for the running of freight trains, so the Great Central needed another route. It therefore formed a partnership with the Great Western Railway to access London via High Wycombe. To do this it constructed a double track main line from a junction at Grendon Underwood to link up with the Great Western at Princes Risborough and by upgrading the line through to High Wycombe. This opened in 1905 and Princes Risborough, which up until then had been on a single track rural branch line, found itself on a main line. Then in 1910 the Great Western built its cut off main line to Birmingham to save 18 and half miles and thus 20 minutes on the route via Reading and Oxford and thereby competing with the London and North Western Railway for Birmingham traffic. It diverged from the Grendon Underwood line at Ashendon Junction, a few miles north of Haddenham. To avoid conflicting movements, the up Great Western line joined via a deviation line and flyover. Princes Risborough thus became an even busier station.

On 20th July 1946, HCC visited the junction and spent some time exploring it and taking photographs. He must have done a bit of walking to get there as it is not very near any road! The first view (opposite page) shows the junction looking north. Straight on and curving to the right is the Great Central Line, while the down Great Western veers off to the left. In the distance is the embankment and flyover where the up Great Western line crosses the Great Central and curves round to the right to join up some way south of the signal box which is behind the camera. The road is signalled for the GC line.

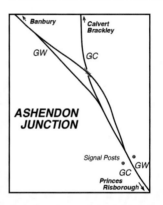

This is the view in the opposite direction looking south, taken from the vicinity of the flyover seen in the background of the previous photo. The down GW main line is on the right, in the middle is the GC and in the left distance you can just make out a signal on the up GW line which has swung round. Sadly this fascinating location did not have a long career as a junction, just 56 years, as the GC closed in 1966. Worse, the GW line was singled in the late 1960s and the flyover was done away with, leaving just the line on the right. With the upturn in fortune under Chiltern Railways, the line was redoubled in 1998. There was obviously no need for a flyover this time as the GC had long been closed and lifted. The flyover girders had been removed. The reinstated up line nonetheless followed the old formation, crossing the GC trackbed on a continuous embankment. This can clearly be seen if you look at the site on Google Earth.

Let's now look at some trains at this location on that day in Summer 1946. We see K3 2-6-0 **2455** (later BR **61964**) coming off the GC route with a southbound goods train, the sort of traffic the line was built for as there was little room for it on the line through Amersham and Rickmansworth. In BR days, 61964 spent nearly ten years at Lincoln and its last four at Doncaster from where it was withdrawn in July 1961. The whole class of 193 powerful 2-6-0s had gone by the end of 1962, the last of them in the great cull of steam locomotives that year.

Coming the other way passing the signal box with northbound coal empties formed of wooden wagons is Austerity 2-8-0 **77430**. We cannot see the signals, but given the type of train and the fact that the loco was based at Woodford Halse, and was one of the 200 that were sold to the LNER (which had absorbed the GC in the 1923 Grouping), it is safe to assume that it was heading onto the GC route! 935 of these locos were built by the War department, based on the Stanier 8F. 733 of them ended up in BR ownership and numbered 90000-90732. They were supposedly an economical design, not intended to last long, yet some lasted to almost the end of BR steam! None of them were preserved, but one of those that remained in Europe after the war has been repatriated from Sweden and is masquerading as the 734th member of the class (90733) and can be found at the Keighley and Worth Valley Railway.

77430 became BR 90040 and spent most of its BR days at Woodford Halse. For its last year it migrated to the North-west and was withdrawn from Rose Grove in July 1965

Now, for balance, a couple of GWR trains. This is a wonderful shot taken on the flyover line of an up express coming over the girders. (No doubt someone can identify train 255.) The GC lines are at right angles underneath.

The loco is also an interesting one. It is Castle Class 4-6-0 **7007 Ogmore Castle**. It entered service in June 1946, so it was only a month old at the time of this photograph. It turned out to be the last of the class constructed by the GWR (British Railways went on to build another 30 of them), so in January 1948 it was renamed **Great Western**. The name Ogmore Castle was actually carried by no less than three of the class: it had previously been carried by 5080 **Defiant** (now preserved at Tyseley, having spent a few years up to 2017 on loan for display at Quainton Road) and finally by BR built 7035. 7007 lasted until February 1963.

Here 0-6-0 pannier tank **5407** is propelling a northbound local auto train service to Banbury. It is scurrying away from the GC route on the sweeping curve which is on a rising gradient (note the gradient post) to meet with the up line. No 5407 remained locally based at Banbury until it ended its career in 1960.

41

Northwards from Moor Park

The Metropolitan Railway was the "mainline" of the London Underground system. Today the Metropolitan Line (as it has become) terminates at Amersham with Chiltern Railways providing services beyond to Aylesbury. However, modern commuters may not be aware that it was once the Metropolitan Railway that used to provide services not only to Aylesbury, but further north through Quainton Road to Verney Junction. They even provided a Pullman dining car for the well-off businessman! Not only that, the line was shared with the Great Central Railway, so express trains to

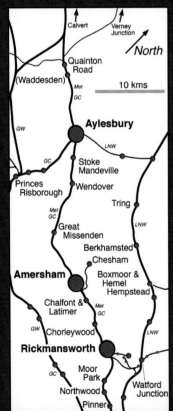

and from Manchester and Sheffield would thunder through to London Marylebone, the most famous of these being *The Master Cutler*. It was all a far cry from the bland procession of Metropolitan S Stock and Chiltern Railways Turbos, efficient though they may be, that we see today!

To attract passengers, the Metropolitan Railway had the bright idea of instead of providing a railway to serve the population, it would provide a population to serve its railway. The plan was to provide very attractive and affordable housing along its route, extolling the virtues of living in the healthy air of the countryside and using their fast and efficient railway to whisk you to and from the City. This was all brilliantly marketed as Metroland, later made all the more famous by Sir John Betjeman.

The scheme was over-ambitious and never reached its full extent and the line north from Aylesbury to Verney Junction closed to passengers as early as 1936. However, the Metropolitan continued to serve stations as far as Aylesbury until 1961. Up until then, electrification only came out as far as Rickmansworth, with trains switching to steam power for the onward journey to Aylesbury, as we shall see. In 1961 the electrification was extended to Chesham and Amersham and services north of Amersham were handed over to British Railways. The Great

Central route was closed on 3rd September 1966, its services having been gradually and deliberately run down for many years. Yet another closure that is now regretted!

The Metropolitan Railway with its varied fleet of distinctive locomotives working a quirky service of goods as well as passenger trains had long been a favourite of HCC and he often visited the line many years before he moved to Berkhamsted. It was one of his "specialist subjects" and he wrote books on it featuring his photos. I have tried to avoid these photos, but as the books are now out of print, it will do no harm if I have inadvertently duplicated some here.

We start at Moor Park on 10th September 1946. Here is a train heading for Rickmansworth, the then limit of electrification, and on the previous page is a train arriving for Baker St. Both consist of Metropolitan Railway T Stock, built in 1927-31 for working from Baker St to Watford and Rickmansworth. When the electrification was extended to Chesham and Amersham in 1961, there was an overlap with deliveries of the replacement A60 stock (so familiar until 2012), so T stock was briefly seen in these places, the last ones going in October 1962. Two cars are preserved and can be seen at The Buckinghamshire Railway Centre at Quainton Road.

The station had originally been called Sandy Lodge after the nearby golf course and, as can be seen in these photos, had rudimentary platform facilities. The line was a two track bottle-neck, carrying Watford and Rickmansworth/Aylesbury local services as well as expresses of the Great Central, now part of the London North Eastern Railway. There had been plans to quadruple the track from Wembley Park to the junction with the Watford line just north of Moor Park, but these were held back by WW2. As can be seen here, work resumed after the war, but was not proceeded with at this stage. It wasn't until 1962 that the scheme was completed, giving Moor Park the four platforms we see today and allowing fast Metropolitan Line trains and those of Chiltern Railways to overtake all-station stopping services.

Also on 10th September 1946, electric locomotive **16 *Oliver Goldsmith*** arrives with an Aylesbury train. It would haul the train one more station as far as Rickmansworth where a steam loco would take over, as we shall see. Note on the left the earlier style of station nameboard that came before the iconic roundel design.

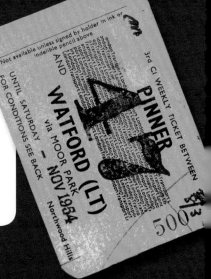

Another of the class 8 Sherlock Holmes, arrives with a Liverpool St train on 29th August 1959, While a train of T stock recedes into the distance. There were 20 of these electric locomotives, constructed by Metropolitan-Vickers in 1922-3 and 16 of them survived in passenger service until 1962 when the A60 stock took over, the other four having been withdrawn earlier after suffering accident damage. They were named after people both real and fictitious, except for number 15 which was named Wembley after being exhibited at the British Empire Exhibition there. It was to be one of the accident-damaged ones and was withdrawn in 1951. Two of the class are preserved: 5 *John Hampden* is at the London Transport Museum and 12 *Sarah Siddons* is in working order and can be seen from time to time on special workings.

Demonstrating the contrast in type of train that could be seen here, one of Sir Nigel Gresley's masterpieces, V2 2-6-2 **4799**, is passing with the 8.20 Manchester to Marylebone express also on 10th September 1946. On the left men are working on the quadrupling of the route which was shortly to be put on hold at this time.

As the Great Central was absorbed into the LNER at the 1923 grouping, it became part of British Railways Eastern Region at Nationalisation in 1948. In 1958 it passed to the London Midland Region and so began a long and painful decline of the main line north of Aylesbury, culminating in closure in 1966. On the loco front, former LMS types began to replace the former LNER ones.

Under the 1946 LNER renumbering scheme the loco became number 828 and as 60828, this locomotive spent its earlier British Railways days alternating between sheds

on the Great Central and the southern part of the East Coast Main Line. In 1958 it moved to York where it spent its last seven years. V2s based in York did still sometimes come south on the GC as far as Woodford Halse, so it may well have kept an association with the line until its end.

We now move to Rickmansworth and see **10 *William Ewart Gladstone*** arriving with the 3.08pm Liverpool Street to Aylesbury. At the station this loco will come off and give way to a steam loco. On the up line the reverse procedure is happening and Fairburn 2-6-4T **42249** is entering the sidings on the left, a site now occupied by a supermarket. The date was 23rd July 1955.

Until the previous March, 42249 had served on the former London Tilbury and Southend line out of Fenchurch Street. It would spend six years on the line here, based at Neasden before being displaced by the extension of the electrification, whereupon it moved on to the Manchester area. It was withdrawn from Bolton in July 1966.

Back on 27th April 1946 the first of the class, **1 *John Lyon***, has arrived at the station with the 1.04pm from Liverpool Street to Aylesbury and is very promptly coming off the train.

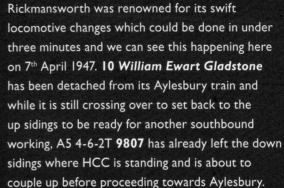

Rickmansworth was renowned for its swift locomotive changes which could be done in under three minutes and we can see this happening here on 7th April 1947. **10 *William Ewart Gladstone*** has been detached from its Aylesbury train and while it is still crossing over to set back to the up sidings to be ready for another southbound working, A5 4-6-2T **9807** has already left the down sidings where HCC is standing and is about to couple up before proceeding towards Aylesbury.

9807 has quickly been attached to the train and is now making a spirited and dramatic departure, probably all the more so for HCC's camera! 9807 was a Robinson Great Central locomotive, designed specifically for working this route and dated back to 1911. These locos were shortly to be replaced by more modern L1 2-6-4 tanks and in February 1950 69807 (as it had become) was moved to Colwick where it lasted until July 1958.

Until 1st November 1937 these trains had been hauled by the Metropolitan Railway's own tank locomotives, but operations were then handed over to the LNER who introduced its own locos. As the Metropolitan locos were non-standard, they had all gone by 1948. From the mid-1950s the former LNER types themselves gave way to former LMS Fairburn designed 2-6-4 tank locomotives as the line was transferred from the Eastern to the London Midland Region.

Two more shots at Rickmansworth of graceful V2 2-6-2s in action. **60863** is passing the signal box with the 3.20pm Marylebone to Manchester on 23rd July 1955. Below Back in LNER days 983 is passing through with the 3.30pm Marylebone to Manchester on 10th September 1946.

60863 was to remain based on the former GC route until it was withdrawn in April 1962. 983 was numerically the last of the class and spent its BR days as 60983 based at Kings Cross. In June 1962 it moved to Grantham but was withdrawn just three months later.

An interesting view from the lineside north of Rickmansworth station on 7th April 1947. It shows the then limit of electrification. In 1961 it was extended to the turnback sidings just north of Amersham station. Note that the sidings here were only partially electrified, to the same point.

A view at Rickmansworth from the platform end looking north on 3rd June 1956 showing the track layout which allowed the swift loco change. In the sidings are Thompson L1 2-6-4T **67781** and Metropolitan 0-4-4T **L48** and on the other side is a train of T stock. This was the occasion of a railtour, "The John Milton Special" which originated at Crystal Palace. L48 is waiting to take over and haul the Rickmansworth-Chesham-Rickmansworth leg of the tour.

P 45

A3 PACIFICS

Introduced in October 1947, the most prestigious train on the line was *The Master Cutler*. Here we see the London–bound service, the 7.40 from Sheffield near Chorleywood on 23rd July 1949 hauled by **60054 *Prince of Wales***. It would have called at Nottingham Victoria and Leicester Central only. (HCC has left it a little late to release the shutter so there is some motion blur, but the photo is of sufficient interest to be included.) In 1958 when the run-down of the GC commenced, this train was re-routed via Retford and the ECML to Kings Cross. 60054 remained a GC loco until 1956 when it was transferred to ECML duties and was withdrawn from New England (Peterborough) in June 1964.

A light load for a Pacific! Here is **2558 *Tracery*** with a short passenger and van train near Great Missenden on 27th May 1939. As **60059,** this loco spent time in the early 1950s on the GC, but with the run-down and transfer of the line to the LMR, it moved to Kings Cross shed from where it would be withdrawn in December 1962.

The 10am from Manchester on 8th July 1939 was hauled by **2552 *Sansovino*** and is seen here near Stoke Mandeville. Note the roof destination boards on the carriages. As **60053** in BR days, the loco left the GC and worked on the Eastern and then North Eastern regions, ending up at Heaton (Newcastle) from where it was withdrawn in May 1963.

METROPOLITAN RAILWAY LOCOMOTIVES

For hauling goods trains and passenger trains on the non-electrified section of the line, the Metropolitan Railway had small fleets of its own locomotives. From 1st November 1937, the locomotives and operation of these services were handed over to the LNER who started to introduce its own locomotives. The Metropolitan locomotives were renumbered into LNER stock. Some of them were transferred to Nottinghamshire to work local services there, but as they were small classes of non-standard design, they were phased out and all had gone by 1948.

They were a particular favourite of HCC and many of his photos of them have been published before. Here are a couple of representative shots, both taken at the same spot north of Chorleywood on 17th August 1935.

K Class 2-6-4T **112** heads a London-bound goods. There were six of this class and their appearance was reminiscent of the 2-6-4Ts of the SR W Class or the LMS Fowler tanks.

For its passenger services the Metropolitan chose locomotives of the relatively rare wheel arrangement of 4-4-4T. Here we see **110**, the last of the class of eight, heading a train to London. It was some engines of this class that were later transferred to Nottinghamshire.

We now move back to Chalfont and Latimer on the 23rd July 1955. Firstly we have a stranger in the camp. A northbound Marylebone line train formed mainly of BR Mk1 stock is headed by BR Standard 4MT **76061**. Now the large BR1B tender gives away the fact that this is in fact a Southern Region locomotive. The larger tender had higher water capacity on a region that had no water troughs. The loco had probably been "borrowed" by Neasden shed after working in off a cross-London working. 76061 was only a month old at the time and was based at Redhill where it stayed until June 1959. It then moved to Eastleigh for the rest of its career and it lasted just into the last year of Southern Region steam, being withdrawn in January 1967.

Chalfont and Latimer was, and still is, the junction for the Chesham Branch and right up to electrification was famous for still using two sets of three ancient "Ashbury" coaches which had been built at the turn of the last century. Until December 1958, when they were replaced by more modern Ivatt 2-6-2 tanks, the locomotives in charge consisted of a pool of three equally elderly Robinson GCR 4-4-2 tanks (67416, 67418 and 67420) dating back to 1903, making this branch a living museum piece. Here we see **67418** having arrived in the bay platform from Chesham on 23rd July 1955 with coaches 513, 515 and 518. Four of the six coaches, including the last two here, have been preserved and beautifully restored on the Bluebell Railway. In recent years they have occasionally been brought back to the London Underground system to work special trains and they have once again been seen here passing through on their way to Amersham.

When the line was electrified, the A60 stock ran as eight-car sets, each made up of two four-car sets which could be split. So this branch (and also the East London Line) ran shuttle trains of four-car A60 stock which continued to use this bay, with through eight-car trains running in the rush hour. However, the S Stock which has replaced the A60s cannot be split, so the London service now runs through to Chesham throughout the day, alternating with trains to Amersham. The bay here is now no longer used.

Here are two more views of the long-lived stock taken pre-nationalisation at Raans Lane near where the Chesham Branch veers away from the main line about a mile north of Chalfont and Latimer station on 30th March 1946. Both the Robinson GCR C13 4-4-2 tanks are in wartime black livery with the economy lettering NE instead of LNER. Above **5193** (later **67418** which we have already seen) heads bunker first towards Chesham, while below **5115** is returning from there. 5115 became **67438** and left the area in 1950 and migrated north and was withdrawn from Leeds in January 1958.

Incidentally, at 3.89 miles, the Chalfont and Latimer-Chesham section is the longest distance between any two London Underground stations.

A lovely view showing plenty of detail at the Chesham terminus on 23rd July 1955 and we see our friend **67418** again, waiting to leave with the 9.17 to Chalfont and Latimer. There was an extensive goods yard beyond the station (now inevitably a car park) and L1 2-6-4T **67760** is on duty there. This Neasden loco, like some of its Metropolitan 4-4-4 T forbears, moved north to Colwick in 1956 and was withdrawn after a short working life of just over a dozen years in 1961.

The station was built as a through one as there were once plans to extend to either Berkhamsted or Tring, something which of course never happened.

The new order. For the last three years before electrification the C13 tanks were replaced by Ivatt 2-6-2 tanks, but still with the Ashbury stock. Here is an example with **41284** waiting to leave for Chalfont and Latimer on 29th August 1959. This loco had been brought down from Skipton and spent a couple of years here before moving down to the West Country at Exmouth Junction in 1961. It spent its last six months at Nine Elms on empty coaching stock workings in and out of Waterloo and made it into the last year of Southern steam, succumbing in March 1967.

Note the station lamps, hand barrow, signal box and extensive advertising hoardings.

The electric rails have been installed and the new turnback sidings to the north of the station have been laid, so we are in the last months of the steam service here. Most of the LMS designed tanks on the line were of the Fairburn variety, but on 25th March 1961 Stanier 2-6-4T **42617** enters Amersham station with the 12.35 Aylesbury to Baker St. After the electrification this loco migrated to the Liverpool area, but only lasted until November 1963 when it was withdrawn from Walton-on-the Hill shed which itself closed a month later.

On the 9th September 1961, London Transport ran a last day Farewell to Steam special from Baker St to Amersham and back. Electric loco 18 **Michael Faraday** did the honours from Baker St to Rickmansworth and Fairburn 2-6-4T **42070**, seen here waiting to depart with the return run, worked to and from Rickmansworth. The fare for the trip was 6/- (30p). HCC was present, but this photo was actually taken by a R F Roberts.

During the year following this, 42070 moved from Neasden to nearby Cricklewood for a time before going to Stoke in July 1964. It was withdrawn from there in June the following year.

Here are a couple of immediate pre-war views taken in the open Chilterns countryside between Great Missenden and Wendover on 8th July 1939. Sandringham "Footballer" B17 **2867** (later **61667**) *Bradford* is heading the 8.20am Manchester to Marylebone express. You can make out the football as part of the nameplate. After 1950 61667 moved to East Anglia and was withdrawn from Cambridge in June 1958.

LNER B3 4-6-0 (formerly GCR 9P Lord Faringdon Class) **6168** was one of only six built in 1917-20 for hauling Great Central expresses. It was named after a GCR director **Lord Stuart of Wortley**. Here it has a more humble task of hauling the 12.42 Aylesbury to Marylebone local service. It was to be the first of the class to be withdrawn, in September 1946. Just one of the six, *Earl Haig*, lasted into BR days as 61497, being withdrawn in April 1949.

AYLESBURY

B1 4-6-0 **1086** is arriving past the south signal box with the 3.20 Marylebone to Manchester on 26th July 1947 in the last six months of the LNER. The background looks far more rural than it does today! The line to Princes Risborough comes in from the right. Then based at Leicester Central, 1086 moved on to Doncaster as 61086 in 1949 and then on to Doncaster and York from where it was withdrawn in the great cull of steam locos in December 1962.

BR Standard 4MT 2-6-4 tank **80117** is taking water before taking the 1.08pm train to Baker St as far as Rickmansworth on a sunny 23rd July 1955. We have a little mystery here. There is no doubt about the number of the loco: it had entered service just two months before-allocated to Whitby! Enlargement shows it is not yet carrying a shed plate, so I can only surmise that, as it was constructed at Brighton, it was loaned to Neasden on its way north. It stayed in the north of England, moving on from Whitby to Leeds and then in 1963 on to Scotland, being withdrawn from Polmadie (Glasgow) in March 1966. So it was certainly a good "cop" for Aylesbury trainspotters to put in their books!

We move to the north end of the station now and enthusiasts are gathering for a last few rides as it is 10th June 1966, less than three months before final closure of the GC route on September 3rd. Local services north of here had finished on 4th March 1963 and all that was left was a sparse semi-fast service to Nottingham and here is Black 5 4-6-0 **44920** on the 2.38 from Marylebone to Nottingham. Most of the locomotives were in a very run down state, but this one went on to serve for another 15 months based at Wigan. At the top of the photo note the flimsy footbridge which takes a public footpath over the line. In recent years this has been replaced with a substantially extended structure with lanes for both pedestrians and cyclists and a lift has been installed.

Looking north from the footbridge now we see another Black 5 4-6-0, **45331**, arriving a year or so earlier with the 8.15 from Nottingham. This one also went on to serve at Wigan until December 1967.

Photo by Rob Freeman

This is not a "past and present" book, but I couldn't resist putting this one in as the changes are so profound! Believe it or not this is the same view as that of 45331 above. It was taken in March 2020 from the rebuilt footbridge and about the only thing in common with the 1965 view is the curvature of the track. 66082 is returning with the empties of one of the daily trains of spoil that run daily from London to be disposed of at the former brick clay pits at Calvert, the surviving most northerly point from London of the GC main line.

On the left instead of green fields is the Chiltern Railways maintenance depot. On the right are a massive car park and the approach road to the station and a supermarket which have replaced the station yard buildings and sidings. Aylesbury is expanding rapidly and to serve the new residential areas being built to the north of the town, Chiltern Railways extended their service to a new station called Aylesbury Vale Parkway which opened on 14th December 2008, so passenger trains do once again traverse these tracks. At the time of writing the go-ahead has just been given for Phase Two of the East-West Rail Link, so hopefully before too long these tracks will become even busier with services to Milton Keynes and Bedford.

On into the Vale of Aylesbury now and here approaching the closed Waddesdon station is A3 Pacific **4473** *Solario* hauling the 3.20 Marylebone to Manchester on 17th June 1939.

This was the unlucky A3. As 60104 based at Kings Cross (it had left the GC in 1957), it was the first to be withdrawn, because of cracked frames, in December 1959, some 16 months before the next one went. The withdrawal of such a prestigious locomotive sent shock waves amongst the enthusiasts of the day, making them realise that the writing really was on the wall for steam power on British Railways.

Looking the other way we see former Metropolitan Railway K class 2-6-4T 114, now in LNER stock as L2 class **6161** still doing the job it was designed for, hauling a goods train towards London on 13th May 1939. The train is passing the remains of Waddesdon Station and what is left of its footbridge. It had closed on 6th July 1936 when Metropolitan services between Aylesbury and Verney Junction ceased. As has been explained earlier, the plans of Metropolitan Railway expansion northwards had proved over-ambitious. Remains of the platform edge can still be seen today.

Here is a rare view of an Aylesbury to Verney Junction train before the service ceased on 6th July 1936.

It is the 11.35 departure from Aylesbury approaching the stop at Waddesdon on 8th April 1933. The locomotive is **8307**, the only one of this small class of twelve F7 locomotives that was fitted for autotrain working. The auto trailer is number 51905 and there is also a cattle wagon, which appears to be occupied, attached to the other end of the locomotive.

These locos had a large cab relative to their size and thereby gained the nickname "Crystal Palace Tanks". This can be clearly seen in this photo of the train returning to Aylesbury. The cattle wagon looks more fully occupied than the passenger coach! All these tank engines had gone by 1948.

The location seen in the first photo may not be that familiar, but the going away shot shows us that we are at Quainton Road, now the headquarters of the Buckinghamshire Railway Centre. Note all the wagons in the yard. The train is the Sundays only 10am Manchester to Marylebone hauled by V2 2-6-2 **4888** on 7th July 1946. Quainton Road was to close to passengers with the cessation of GC local services north of Aylesbury on 4th March 1963. Just before the bridge in the distance is the junction where the Great Central joined the Metropolitan Railway and the latter's line to Verney Junction used to pass under the right-hand arch of the bridge.

As 60917 the loco spent its entire British Railways career based at Doncaster, apart from spending the summer of 1953 as one of the locos on loan to the Southern Region to cover for the Merchant Navy Pacifics while they were temporarily withdrawn for axle inspections following the fracture of one of them at speed. 60917 was withdrawn in April 1962.

Watford

Watford Junction was, and still is, a major station on the West Coast Main Line. As well as its main line and commuter services, there were branches to Croxley Green, Rickmansworth Church Street and St Albans Abbey. It was also the terminus of the third and fourth rail DC suburban lines, with frequent trains throughout the day to Euston and Broad Street, as well as to Elephant and Castle on the Bakerloo Line. There was a steam depot, coded 1C, alongside the up slow line at the north end of the station and a footbridge (demolished when the line was electrified) connecting the main line platforms gave a grandstand view of this. The Casserleys certainly took full advantage of it! There was a large carriage shed round the corner alongside the St Albans branch and a large goods yard.

Looking through the Casserley collection, it is obvious that both HCC and RMC would sometimes step back a train here on their commute to and from work in order to take a few photographs. At the time you could only do this in the peak, as the local service north of Watford was very sparse at other times. Indeed, before electrification there were only as many services all day as there are now in less than a couple of hours!

There are now also services to East Croydon via the West London Line. London Overground works the DC Line services to Euston, joining in with the Bakerloo Line from Harrow and Wealdstone to Queen's Park southwards.

Today the branches to Croxley Green, Rickmansworth and the services to Broad Street have long gone and the Bakerloo Line now terminates at Harrow and Wealdstone, but the St Albans branch remains and the frequency of commuter services to London is at a higher level than it has ever been.

However, unlike the main line commuter services which have mushroomed, there are actually far fewer trains on the Harrow to Watford section than there were in the past. When the main line was electrified in the 1960s, the carriage shed and the steam shed closed, the site of the latter has become the inevitable station car park.

However, the yard still sees regular freight traffic to an aggregates terminal. One major disappointment is that, despite its being mooted off and on for several years, the proposed link-up between the Metropolitan Line and the former Croxley Green branch has never got off the ground.

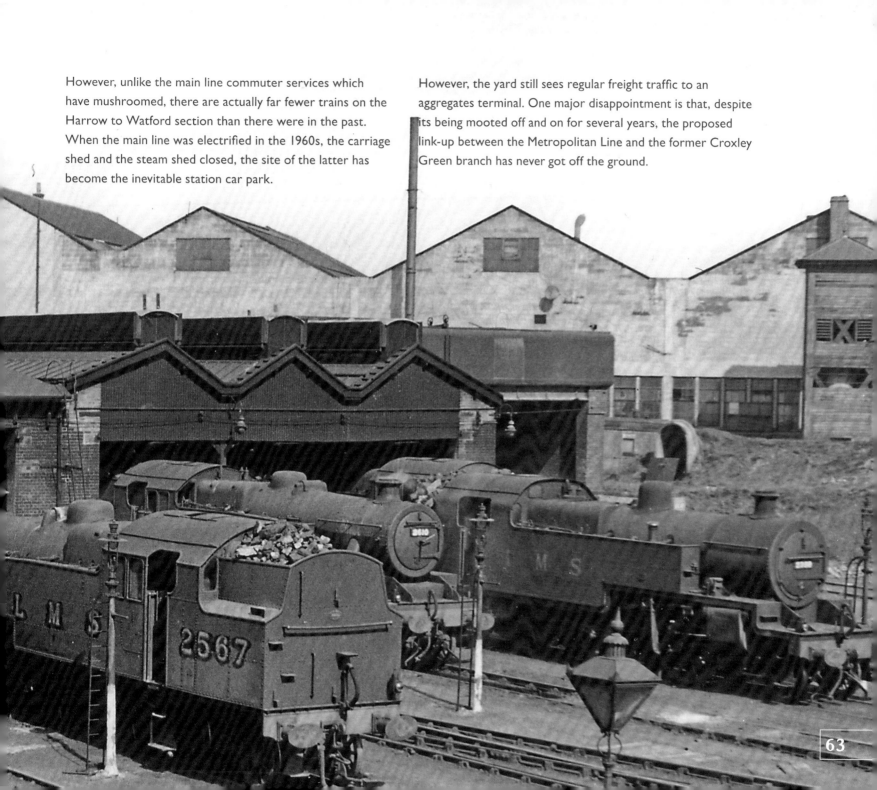

The previous page shows a view of the shed from the station footbridge in LMS post war days with 2P 4-4-0 **672**, Stanier 2-6-4Ts **2567** and **2610** and Fowler 2-6-4T **2389** on show on a sunny 7th April 1947.

672, of a type not that common on this stretch of the WCML, spent its whole life at Shed IC as the Engineer's Watford pet loco. When not required for Engineer's duties, 672, later 40672, could be found on local pick up goods or on local passenger

trains. It lasted until October 1962. The tank engines were more nomadic in British Railways days and spent time at several depots. 42567 had moved on to other areas of the WCML by the time of nationalisation and ended its days in Manchester at Patricroft in March 1965. 42610 also moved on in 1948, finishing at Barrow in April 1966. 42389 spent more time at Watford until it moved on to the Stoke area and was withdrawn from Speke Junction in March 1963.

Stanier 2-6-4T **2600** arrives on the up slow under a magnificent LNWR signal gantry with the 3.35 from Rugby to Euston on 9th September 1946. The smoky Jinty on shed is **7359**. There is also a passenger train receding on the down main. 42600, as it became, was based at Bletchley until August 1952 when it moved to Stoke. It remained there for 10 years until it was withdrawn in November 1962. In British Railways days, 47359 was at Camden until moving north to Stafford (via a short spell at Coventry) in 1955. It was withdrawn from there in July 1965.

Black 5 4-6-0 **45003** arrives at Watford Junction on a lovely sunny morning with the Saturdays-only 8.00am Northampton to Euston on the 13th August 1949. It is on the up slow passing the shed and going under the magnificent old LNWR signal gantry.

HCC had this Saturday off and took this photograph on his way to taking young Richard to explore the London Tilbury and Southend lines. 45003 was based at Rugby at the time and moved to Willesden in 1953 for a couple of years before going to Crewe and then finally Stoke, where it lasted until as late as May 1967.

This is an old postcard from circa 1920, published by Loosely and Sons of Berkhamsted, giving a marvellous view of the layout of the station looking north. There are wagons in the goods yard as you would expect, but otherwise there is a distinct lack of trains on view, the loco shed yard is empty and the streets around are virtually devoid of traffic!

At the bottom of the photograph the signal box stands out. On the west side are the four platforms of the New Line (now the Overground platforms) with its long platform 5 whose track extends behind and beyond the down fast platform 6. The footbridge connecting the main line platforms 6-9 can be seen at their north end. The St Albans platforms curve round to the right and the loco shed is just north of the station on the east side. The current St Albans platform is where the north bit of the yard was then and the modern aggregates terminal occupies the land just beyond the yard sidings seen here on the right.

WATFORD FROM THE AIR.   JUNCTION AND SURROUNDINGS

COPYRIGHT 2

As it was on 28th July 1956 on the DC lines, today served by London Overground. One of the LNWR Oerlikon sets which were built for the start of electric trains on the line is in platform 2 with a Euston bound train. It was coming to the end of its working life, as the BR built Class 501s (as they became) would start to appear the following year. In platform 3 is a Bakerloo Line train of 1938 stock which has presumably just arrived, as it is still showing Watford in the destination indicator. At this time there was a frequent service of Euston, Broad Street and Bakerloo Line trains throughout the day. The line had a special signalling system which allowed trains to run very closely one behind the other at peak times.

A dramatic low angle shot of 4-4-0 **41167** as it gets away from platform 6, the down fast, with the 3.05pm Euston to Rugby on 16th August 1958. By this date these Midland Compounds were quite a rare sight on the WCML and indeed 41167, then Rugby based, was withdrawn just two months later. On the left is the siding extension of the now long gone platform five. The north end of the platform and this siding were often used for stabling DC line units or Bakerloo Line trains.

Five years later electrification work is underway, the A412 St Albans Road bridge has been raised and rebuilt and the siding has gone. Jubilee 4-6-0 **45601 British Guiana**, of Newton Heath shed, leaking steam from every orifice, also makes a dramatic departure from platform 6 with the 11.55 Euston to Crewe on 21st December 1963. 45601 had been a local Camden loco until September 1959 when it moved to Willesden, then on to Newton Heath, Manchester in June 1960 from where it was withdrawn in September 1964.

Two splendid views of the unique 4-6-2 Turbomotive **46202** as it restarts the 8.30 Euston to Liverpool on 13th August 1949. Unlike many other one-offs, this was a relatively successful one (though it did have extended periods out of service for maintenance) and was in service from 1935 until 1949, so this would've been one of its last workings before a turbine failure caused its withdrawal. Pictures of it in BR livery are not that common, so this is yet another real gem from the Casserley collection.

It was subsequently rebuilt as a very handsome conventional locomotive, a sort of hybrid between a Princess and a Duchess, and having been named **Princess Anne**, it entered service in 1952, only to be destroyed a couple of months later in the Harrow disaster.

A photograph, taken from the old footbridge that was later swept away by the electrification of the line, that is as fascinating for the fashion detail of the passengers of the period as it is for the railway interest! Note how many people are wearing hats. According to his diary, HCC was on his way to the cinema-taking his camera with him!

Fowler 2-6-4T **42316** and un-rebuilt Patriot 4-6-0 **45538** *Giggleswick* are arriving with the 4.15 Euston to Bletchley on 14th April 1949. The pilot was hitching a ride to Watford, probably to save a light engine move, so was to come off here. In the background a coach of a St Albans branch train can be seen.

42316 was a local Willesden IA loco having short spells away at Crewe, Warwick and Neasden in the 1950s before finally moving away to Stockport in June 1958 and was withdrawn from there in February 1963. 45538 had come down from Leeds (more appropriate for its name!) to Willesden in August 1948 and would move north to Liverpool Edge Hill in the month after this photo was taken. It then went to Preston in July 1957 and then came back to Willesden in June 1959 before moving on to Nuneaton in January 1961. None of the un-rebuilt members of the class survived the great cull of 1962 and this one was withdrawn in the September of that year.

Also seen from the vantage point of the footbridge, Fowler 2-6-4T **42389,** now in early British Railways livery, basks in the spring sunshine on its home shed on 14th April 1949. A former LNWR 0-8-0 just gets into the shot. The St Albans branch runs behind the signal box and then to the left of the carriage shed in the background and the signals controlling the approach to the station can be seen in the middle distance.

Moving on three years to the 28th June 1952 and the signal box has been replaced and relocated a bit further north. The signals appear to be the same though. Two visiting engines are on shed: ex LNWR 0-8-0 **48927** from Nuneaton and Black 5 **45149** from Stoke. 48927 would be withdrawn from Liverpool Edge Hill in November 1961 and 45149 lasted almost to the very end of BR steam, being withdrawn from Lostock Hall shed near Preston in June 1968.

Fowler 2-6-2T LMS **4** on a crisp winter morning is manoeuvring around the shed yard. Because of the cramped layout, locomotives coming on and off shed had to reverse in this headshunt. The St Albans branch platforms are on the right. It is 28th January 1948, barely a month into the British Railways era, so the loco is still in full LMS livery and yet to be renumbered 40004. It has been said that this class didn't quite look right with their small diameter boiler and smokebox and they seemed under powered, yet they put in 30 years' useful service, so they can't have been that bad!

This loco was about to move from Watford 1C to the main shed Willesden 1A, so it was still a local loco until it moved away north in October 1956. It ended its days at Heaton Mersey in November 1959.

3rd-SINGLE SINGLE
Croxley Green   Oroxley
Croxley Green   Watfo
Watford West
544
WATFORD WEST
(M) -/2 N   FARE -/2
For conditions see over For conditi

THE ELECTRIFIED BRANCHES

A three-car Oerlikon set (so-called after the Swiss company that supplied the electrical equipment) arrives at Rickmansworth Church St on 25th August 1951. The branch, opened on 1st October 1862, would close to passengers a few months later on 3rd March 1952, though freight lingered on until 2nd January 1967. These units were withdrawn between 1957 and 1960: they were replaced by the BR Eastleigh-built units of class 501.

One motor coach, No 28249, of these units survives and is preserved in the NRM at York. Unfortunately every time I've been to see it, it has been tucked away and you could only see it from floor level, so the spacious and luxurious (by today's standards!) seating area shown in these photos was not visible.

Two views inside Oerlikon stock: Third Class above and former First Class area below.

Below: Another Oerlikon three-car set stands at Croxley Green, the other DC branch line from Watford, on 23rd June 1952. There were once peak hour through services from Euston and Broad St, but when the east to south curve at Bushey was closed, these ceased and the service became a shuttle from Watford. Despite half-hearted attempts to promote the line, it went into decline and by the end in 1996 there was just one

early morning parliamentary train per day! A road widening scheme which breached the embankment was the final nail in the coffin. There has been much talk over the years of linking the nearby Metropolitan Line into this branch (it could be useful for serving Watford General Hospital and Watford FC's Vicarage Road ground for example) and running Met trains into Watford Junction, but sadly nothing has ever come of it.

THE ST ALBANS ABBEY BRANCH

Ivatt 2-6-2T **41220** waits to depart with a train to St Albans Abbey on a beautiful spring evening on 30th April 1955.

41220 entered service as a British Railways loco in September 1948, briefly allocated to Crewe before coming south to Watford. It yo-yoed between there and various sheds further north throughout the 1950s until finally moving away to Crewe North in May 1958 and was withdrawn from Stockport Edgeley in November 1966.

Fowler 2-6-2T **43** arrives at St Albans Abbey with the 6pm from Watford Jct on 11th August 1945. With the end of the war in Europe, HCC was starting to get out and about again with his camera!

Apart from a very short spell allocated to Bangor, as 40043, this loco remained a 1C local and was withdrawn from Willesden, where it had been for the last year of its life, in November 1959.

Another view of 43, now **40043,** as it propels the 7.48pm to Watford Jct out of the St Albans Abbey terminus on 19th July 1954.

The RCTS "Hertfordshire Railtour" at St Albans Abbey on 30th April 1955. This tour did a circuit of branch lines to the north west of London. J52 0-6-0 saddle tank **68878** has brought in the train from Hatfield on this leg of the tour. The branch from Hatfield to St Albans Abbey had closed to passengers on 28th September 1951, but would remain open on part of the line from the Hatfield end for freight until December 1968. 68878 was a Kings Cross loco which was withdrawn a year later in May 1956.

On the other end of the train is ex-LNWR 0-8-0 **49431,** then based at Rugby, which would take the train to Watford Jct where tour participants would temporarily change trains to do a trip to Rickmansworth Church St and back before continuing in this train back to London.

Below: One of Stanier's masterpieces, Pacific **6237** **City of Bristol** on the 8.20 from Carlisle to Euston on 26th April 1947. The locomotive is in its de-streamlined state with the sloping smokebox which had been necessary to accommodate the streamline casing. It was this that gave the nickname "Semi" that many spotters used for the class, (though not this compiler, who called them "Coros"). The name stuck even after they had all been rebuilt with full smokeboxes and despite the fact that 14 of the 38-strong class were never streamlined! Nowadays of course "Duchess" is what is most commonly used for the preserved examples. Also of interest on the left is the pair of LMS sets stabled in Platform 5. These had been built in two batches in 1926 and 1932 to supplement the Oerlikons. They were of a similar design to the LMS units that worked from Manchester to Altrincham (though those used the overhead system of electrification.) They lasted a little longer into 1963, latterly only appearing mainly in the rush hour.

All the Royal Scot Class and eighteen of the Patriots were rebuilt with new tapered type 2A boilers, but only two of the 191 Jubilees were so treated. Here we see one of them, **5735 Comet**, coming out of the murk of the original Watford tunnel on an up express on 20th March 1947. All the rebuilds were fitted with distinctive smoke deflectors, but initially they were released without them as seen here. The enlarged boiler can therefore be more readily appreciated. It was a local 1B Camden loco at the time. After a short spell in the North West in 1960, 45735 returned to 1A Willesden and then moved on to Annesley to work remaining former Great Central main line semi fasts for the last year of its working life, so it would have been seen on another line through the Chilterns. It was withdrawn in October 1964.

From 1954 onwards, British Railways began the mass introduction of Diesel Multiple Units to replace steam power on suburban and branch line work. However, ahead of this, in 1952, British United Traction built three prototype railcars, two power cars with a centre trailer, as a private speculative venture. These were tested on a number of branch lines around the country, including on the Watford Junction to St Albans Abbey line. They were eventually purchased by British Railways and a further eight cars were built. From 1955 until 1958 they were a regular sight on the St Albans Abbey branch. They were notoriously rough-riding and had the rather unkind nickname "The Flying Bricks".

They had the advantage, as seen here, that they could work as three-, two- or single-coach trains according to traffic demands. The original three cars needed modifications before entering service and the set is seen here in the yard at Watford Junction on 30th April 1955, newly repainted into green from its original two-tone grey livery with red lining, presumably on a test run before regular service started in the following July. The original three cars numbered M79740M-M79742M were easily distinguished by their skirting covering the wheels, which the later-built cars did not have. The second view shows M79742M about to work solo to St Albans on 15th March 1956.

L. M. & S. R
FOR CONDITIONS SEE NOTICES
NAVY ARMY & AIR FORCE on FURLOUGH
LONDON (EUSTON) TO
WATFORD (HIGH ST. JUNC, or WEST)
OR CASHEY GREEN
FARE 1/4 c

Snow!

There's something magical about trains in the snow, particularly steam ones. In the first book, Richard Casserley spoke about the severe winter of 1947 and about the particularly heavy falls of snow in the nights of 6th and 7th March that year. Some spectacular photos were included in the book and I wanted to see if there were any more. I was not disappointed! It appears that HCC spent those two days firstly at the lineside just north of his home up to the Northchurch Tunnel approaches and then at the north end of the tunnel. However, according to his diary, he was in the middle of spending eleven weeks off work with bronchitis, so going out in these conditions would not have helped his recovery! Here is a selection of the photos he took, including some taken on other occasions.

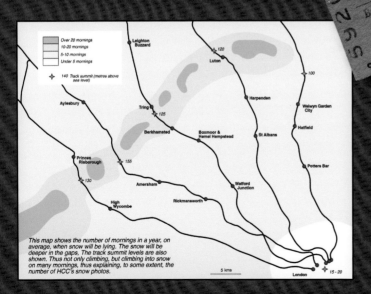

This map shows the number of mornings in a year, on average, when snow will be lying. The snow will be deeper in the gaps. The track summit levels are also shown. Thus not only climbing, but climbing into snow on many mornings, thus explaining, to some extent, the number of HCC's snow photos.

This photo shows just how bad the conditions were on 6th March 1947! Jubilee 4-6-0 **5666 Cornwallis** has obviously encountered some very deep snow on its journey to London with an up express. RMC spoke about the heavy delays, but from the number of photos that HCC took, the trains did at least manage to keep running.

Except for a month allocated to Willesden in December 1960, *Cornwallis* spent its British Railways career based at sheds in Birmingham, Crewe, Liverpool, Carlisle and finally Warrington, from where it was withdrawn in April 1965. It was nonetheless a common visitor to the London area and 45666 is one I remember seeing here as a young spotter.

B.R. (M.) 3rd CLASS WEEKLY SEASON
For Conditions see back   Rate
Available between   26 3 J
EUSTON (50.) & BERKHAMSTE
38
UNTIL
17 SEP 55
R.M. Cassley
Sign here in full

The snow has completely covered the tracks in Berkhamsted goods yard and the wagons of coal for the gas works seem isolated. With its wheels encrusted in snow, 0-6-0 **4443** scurries through light engine on the up slow on 6th March 1947. From the way the exhaust is being blown, there is a strong wind coming from the north east, so it must've been bitterly cold!

(4)4443 was a local Watford engine until May 1956 when it moved north to Barrow, where it stayed for the rest of its career which ended in August 1965.

Seen from the same spot the same day is Fowler 2-6-4T **2344**, also with snow round its wheels, with an up local. By the next year it had moved on to the Stoke area, from where it was withdrawn as 42344 in May 1961.

Two locos for just 8 coaches! HCC has moved closer to the wagons for this shot of Royal Scot 4-6-0 **6150** *The Life Guardsman* piloting Jubilee 4-6-0 **5722** *Defence* on this working on the up fast. The sixth vehicle is interesting, possibly a Travelling Post Office coach.

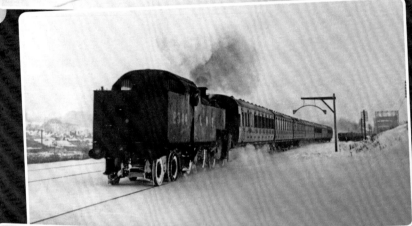

6150 has been rebuilt with a taper boiler, but is yet to receive its distinctive smoke deflectors. As 46150, it was to move all around WCML sheds in its BR days, finishing at Carlisle Kingmoor in November 1963. 45722 also moved around before spending six months at the Rugby Test Plant from September 1956. It was then based locally at London sheds and was condemned back at Rugby in December 1962, the month there was a mass cull of steam locomotives. So many were withdrawn in fact, that The Railway Magazine stated that it was too many for them to list their individual details as it usually did.

Going by the photos I have seen, HCC actually took relatively few at Berkhamsted station itself, preferring the lineside just to the north, from opposite his house and on to Northchurch Tunnel or the view from his house *Ravensbourne* for his local photos. That said, here is a cracking shot taken when he was standing in front of the signal box of 8F 2-8-0 **8114** approaching the station with a long train of northbound empties returning home to the Midlands coal fields on 24th February 1947. Such workings made freight locomotives based at sheds in the Midlands a common sight at Berkhamsted in steam days. Just past the magnificent tall signals (to improve sighting from the

trains coming out of the cutting on a curve) is the site of the original station, whose goods yard was opposite the snow covered cutting seen in the background. It can be seen that at that time there was a connection from the goods yard sidings out to the fast lines as well as (out of sight behind HCC) to the slow lines.

(4)8114 was a long-term resident of Kirkby in Ashfield shed until it moved to Wigan Springs Branch in December 1964 where it lasted until April 1967.

A wartime snow scene viewed from HCC's study at *Ravensbourne* across the garden on 9th January 1945. Ex LNWR 0-8-0 **9150** passes through a very snowy Berkhamsted with a southbound goods. All Saints Church stands out in the background. This class of locomotive did long service on the WCML and this particular one moved away to the North-west division in 1949 and was withdrawn from there ten years later as 49150.

On the same day a goods on the up fast is double headed by 8F 2-8-0 **8618** and Black 5 4-6-0 **5343**. Neither loco was local, but both survived into 1967, almost to the end of steam.

A spectacular broadside shot of a snow encrusted 8F 2-8-0 **8679** with an up goods passing Berkhamsted yard on 6th March 1947, viewed from *Ravensbourne*. (4)8679 was a local Willesden engine until October 1954 when it moved away to various sheds and was withdrawn from Lostock Hall shed near Preston in October 1966.

And another 8F, **8110** going the other way on a down goods on 9th January 1945. In 1950 48110, as it had now become, moved to the Western Region and served at Bristol and Shrewsbury for a dozen years, before returning to the London Midland Region at Stoke for three years or so and was withdrawn in July 1967.

A British Railways era shot now. The North Wind doth blow again as Jubilee 4-6-0 **45584**, perhaps appropriately named **North West Frontier**, puts up a spectacular exhaust while hauling an express through Berkhamsted on the down slow on Sunday 9th March 1958. The headcode suggests that this is a special of some sort. The locomotive was a long term resident of Blackpool shed at the time. It was withdrawn from Carlisle Kingmoor in October 1964.

Back to the winter of 1947 and a little closer to the station, 8F 2-8-0 **8630** is heading some more northbound empty wooden coal wagons past the distinctive down starter signal on the 23rd February. Behind the crane in the yard is a distinctive line of mainly horse chestnut trees which is still there today. 8630 was a local Willesden loco at the time, but the next year it moved north to the Crewe and   Liverpool areas where it spent its British Railways career as 48630 until it was withdrawn from Crewe South in July 1965.

An up local headed by Fairburn 2-6-4T **42673** has just come through Northchurh Tunnel on 9th March 1958. It was a Rugby based loco at the time and after moving around the London Midland Region finished its career at Barrow in August 1965.

When he took over as CME of the LMS, Fairburn modified Stanier's design of these tank engines and this was the very first of them, following on immediately numerically from the Stanier locos.

We now move to the north of Northchurch Tunnel. Rebuilt Patriot 4-6-0 **5526 *Morecambe and Heysham*** heads a down express on what is now a crisp clear day with lying snow, 7th March 1947. Steam can be seen in the background still billowing out of the tunnel.

5526 was one of 18 of the Patriot Class to be rebuilt with a taper boiler, which made it difficult at a casual glance to distinguish them from the Royal Scots. It is seen here in smart LMS black livery with straw lining. It has not yet received its curved smoke deflectors, although this shot doesn't show any need for them! It was based at Liverpool Edge Hill, but in British Railways days, as 45526, it was a long term resident of Carlisle Upperby, from where it was withdrawn in October 1964.

Looking north away from the tunnel we see Black 5 4-6-0 **4968** with an up express on 7th March 1947. The nice fluffy exhaust of condensed steam in the cold air is once again being carried away by a north-east wind. 4968 would shortly no longer be seen in our area, as in a year's time it would be transferred to Scotland and would spend the whole of its British Railways career as 44968 allocated to Glasgow area sheds. It was withdrawn from Motherwell in June 1964.

Rebuilt Royal Scot 4-6-0 **6129 *The Scottish Horse*** is seen from the banks of the frozen Grand Union Canal heading a down express away from the tunnel on 7th March 1947. Like its classmates at the time it was still to be fitted with curved smoke deflectors. As 46129, it was only briefly allocated to Willesden in 1957, but would nonetheless often work to Euston from various London Midland Region sheds. It was withdrawn from Longsight in June 1964.

A respectably clean 8F 2-8-0 **8200** heads an up mixed goods, again in the snow scene on 7th March 1947. (4)8200 would remain a long term resident of Toton for the next ten years and then after stints at Staveley Barrow Hill, Edge Hill and Newton Heath, it just made it into the last year of steam, being withdrawn from Bolton in January 1968.

St Albans

We have already briefly visited St Albans Abbey station in the section on Watford, but here are some views taken at the main station, St Albans City, on the Midland Main Line (MML) from St Pancras to the Midlands, Sheffield, and, as it was back then, to Leeds, the Settle and Carlisle and to Manchester. The MML didn't feature the more glamorous locomotive classes, perhaps dating back to Midland Railway days when they had a small engine policy. The line was more known for the endless procession of coal trains heading to and from the Midlands coalfields to supply the Capital. The mainstay of express power in the period we are covering was the Stanier Jubilee class, though Royal Scots and Britannias did make an appearance in the last years of steam on the line before the Peak Class diesels took over.

Let's start with a couple of local trains arriving, long before the days of Thameslink! Firstly here is Stanier 2-6-4T **2479** with the 6pm train from St Pancras to Harpenden on 23rd August 1947. This was a local 14C St Albans engine and remained only until June 1949 when as 42479 it moved on to the Stoke, Liverpool and Manchester areas. It was re-allocated back down south to 1E Bletchley in September 1961, but was withdrawn a month later.

Fowler 2-6-2T **40039** is approaching the station on the 5.56pm from Moorgate on a sunny evening on 19th July 1954. This was one of twenty (40021-40040) of the seventy locos in this class to be fitted with condensing apparatus to reduce emissions while working in the tunnels in London on this route. It remained a local 14C locomotive right up to its withdrawal in December 1959.

One of the original Midland Railway 3-cylinder 4-4-0 Compounds (put simply, meaning it had one inside high pressure cylinder and two outside low pressure ones) approaches the station with what looks like a special working on 23rd August 1947. 1002 then had less than a year left in service as it was to be withdrawn from Nottingham shed in June 1948. The doyen of the class 1000 has been preserved as part of the National Collection and is currently (2020) on loan as a static exhibit to Barrow Hill Roundhouse.

At the same location, but viewed from between the two sets of running lines, is Jubilee Class 4-6-0 **5585** *Hyderabad* hauling the 5.32pm express from St Pancras to Nottingham on the same day, 23rd August 1947.

As 45585 this locomotive spent time allocated to various sheds for passenger workings all over the former Midland Railway system and was withdrawn in May 1964 from Derby.

Two more 4-4-0 Compounds now, of the later LMS Fowler type, eking out their last years in service on semi-fast passenger trains. They are both working the same train, but some five years apart, the 4.22 pm (though RMC's notes say in 1947 departure was a minute earlier at 4.21) Leicester to St Pancras. Above we see **40931** pulling away nicely on 14th June 1952 and below **1117** on 23rd August 1947. **1117** went first, being withdrawn as 41117 from the former Midland Railway shed at Gloucester Barnwood in April 1955. 40931 spent its last few months away from its native Midland, being withdrawn from Lancaster in October 1958.

The Compounds were a particular favourite of the Casserleys, so I've made a point of including some here. Note also the backing boards to the signal arms to improve sighting on the down fast in the top photo. To the rear of the train you can just make out the signal box which has now been preserved as a museum. The Group which run this have confirmed the following:

The rather strange "hut on a pole" seen behind the loco was the water tower and softening plant of the loco shed. This was necessary because the hard water to be found in the Chilterns would, if left untreated, cause undue deposits to build up in the pipework and boiler tubes of the locomotives.

23rd August 1947 again and the sun has now come out! Jubilee 4-6-0 **5616 *Malta*** is on the 1.50 Manchester Central (now the Manchester Central Convention Centre, formerly known as the GMex Centre) to St Pancras express. The loco became **45616 *Malta*** GC in September 1948, as the whole Island had uniquely been awarded the George Cross in honour of the heroic wartime exploits of the Islanders. It was a long term resident of 14B Kentish Town, but spent its last couple of years moving around Nottingham, Leicester and Manchester. It was withdrawn from Leicester in January 1961, one of the earlier ones of the class to go.

Note that 5616 is running with a small Fowler tender which gives it an odd appearance, made worse by the unfortunate juxtaposition of the chimneys of the loco shed behind. Even the great photographers do not always get it quite right every time!

It's the 4.22pm Leicester to St Pancras again, this time headed by Black 5 4-6-0 **44817** on 19th July 1954. 44817 was another long term resident of Kentish Town. In 1962 it moved on to Burton, Bolton, Manchester and finally in October 1966 to Carlisle Kingmoor where it lasted until August 1967.

With St Albans being the destination of many of the commuter trains, a locomotive shed was needed here to service the steam locos that worked them. It was situated to the south of the station on the east side. Here Fowler 2-6-2T **38**, another of the class fitted with condensing apparatus, is seen during an RCTS visit on 1st February 1936 by the coaling stage. This loco spent its life based locally at either Kentish Town or Cricklewood and was withdrawn in July 1961.

Here we see **161** on shed, an example of the Stanier version of the 2-6-2T, again on 23rd August 1947. It was considered to be one of his less successful designs, yet some members of the class lasted until the end of 1962. This one became 40161 and had an interesting last few years: it remained locally at Kentish Town until April 1952 when it moved to Wales, to Abergavenny. In September 1958 it was put into store, but was reactivated in July 1960 at Bristol Barrow Road. It moved on to Templecombe on the Somerset and Dorset three months later in October, but it obviously wasn't appreciated there, as it was withdrawn in the December of that year.

We have already seen 2-6-2T **39** in BR days as 40039 arriving on a commuter train from London, but here it is in the shed yard with a crane in the background in LMS days as plain **39** on 1st February 1936. This is another shot taken during an RCTS visit to the shed.

In early BR days Fowler 2-6-4T **42334** is on shed on 12th June 1950. It bears no mark of ownership and the style of number characters is a sort of cross between LMS and BR. The loco was in the middle of a six year stay on this, its home shed at the time. It later served in Birmingham, came south again, then moved via a spell at Leicester to Manchester and was withdrawn from Trafford Park in December 1965, the third last of the 125-strong class to go. With the introduction of Diesel Multiple Units (later Class 127) from 1959, there was no further need for this shed and it closed on 11th January 1960.

We now move to the station itself and Fairburn 2-6-4T **42134** has arrived with the 10.20 from St Pancras on 12th June 1950. It remained a local engine until displaced by dieselisation in November 1961 when it moved to Manchester. In June 1965 it went on to Barrow and then spent its last few months from December 1966 until the following April based at Tebay for banking trains up the famous climb to Shap Summit.

Looking the other way we see Fowler 2-6-4T **42341** waiting to leave with the Saturdays-only 8.47 to St Pancras on 27th March 1954. Presumably the stock has arrived on an incoming service and instead of being shunted is to depart directly south from this down platform. 42341 had been a 14C St Albans loco since April 1951 and would remain there until withdrawn in October 1959. Unlike 42334 which we saw on shed and which was one of the last, this one was one of the first to go.

We now move to the north end of the station. Jubilee Class 4-6-0 **45590** *Travancore* is about to pass through with the 7.15am Manchester to St Pancras on 12th June 1950. Note the roof destination board on the first coach. 45590 did stints at various Midlands, Sheffield and Manchester sheds before spending its last two years based in Warrington. It was withdrawn in December 1965.

Here's a real long distance train and what a route it would have taken! It's the 9.54pm sleeper from Edinburgh which would have come via the much lamented Waverley route (which was to close in 1969) and then the Settle and Carlisle line to Leeds where it would have picked up this Leeds Holbeck based locomotive, another Jubilee Class 4-6-0 **45566** *Queensland*. The date is 27th March 1954. 45566 would spend the whole of its BR career at Holbeck and be withdrawn in November 1962 when displaced by Peak Class diesels.

This is a very unusual pairing of locos on another long London-bound fitted goods approaching the station on that sunny 27th March 1954. A modern Ivatt Class 4 2-6-0 **43049** is piloting a much older LMS Compound 4-4-0 **41083**.

On 3rd December 1946 a decidedly grubby (though it looks as if the buffer beam has had a fresh coat of red paint) Stanier 8F 2-8-0 **8076** plods through on what is probably a very long goods train bound for London. Note the style of station nameboard. 8076 was based in the Midlands at Westhouses at the time, but in February 1951 as 48076 it would move to the Wakefield area on the then North Eastern Region where it would spend the rest of its long life, not being withdrawn until November 1967.

162 of the Ivatts were built, but only 3 of them had appeared for the LMS by Nationalisation. In fact the majority were ordered by BR for service on the Eastern and North Eastern Regions! 43049 looks ungainly with the double chimney that was fitted to the first 50 of the class (so this is the last of them) and it turned out that, rather than improve performance, the double chimney actually hindered it, so they were quickly replaced with single ones which improved the look of the locos. 43049 was based at 17A Derby at the time and in June 1956 it moved on to Birmingham (Saltley), Manchester (Heaton Mersey) and finally Carlisle Kingmoor in November 1964. It was withdrawn in August 1967. One of the class (43106) entered preservation straight out of service and can be seen in action on the Severn Valley Railway.

41083 was also a Derby 17A loco at the time and lasted there for another four and a half years before being withdrawn in December 1958.

Welwyn and Potters Bar

Readers who travel regularly on the East coast Main Line (ECML) will know of the bottleneck north of Welwyn Garden City where the four tracks are reduced to two to cross Digswell Viaduct and go through the two tunnels after Welwyn North station. This can often cause delays to services. However, younger readers may be unaware that until 1959 there was a similar two-track bottleneck through the three tunnels at Hadley Wood and Potters Bar. As we shall see, HCC spent some glorious sessions south of Potters Bar Tunnel when it was still double track.

A note on the LNER loco numbers that we shall see in these pages: until 1946 the numbering of LNER locos was quite chaotic, with locos of the same class carrying totally different number series from their classmates, depending on which batches they had been built in. In 1946 it was decided it was high time to streamline the numbering system. This had only just got underway with a few locos renumbered, when a further revision was decided upon, meaning that some locos ended up being renumbered twice. This explains the number 502 displayed by Flying Scotsman at the National Railway Museum in York a few years ago which mystified some people. It had carried this number from January to May 1946 only.

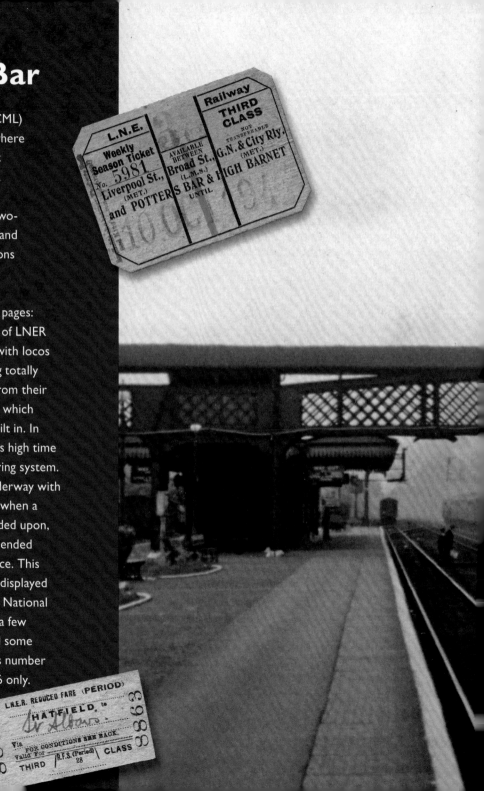

However we begin at Welwyn Garden City firmly in the BR era on 26th May 1956. One of Flying Scotsman's A3 Pacific classmates, **60062 *Minoru***, is rushing through with a heavy northbound express. An everyday scene back then, but regular steam had only seven more years left here. Based at Top Shed (Kings Cross) at the time, this loco continued to serve on the southern part of the ECML and was withdrawn from New England shed in Peterborough in December 1964.

This appears to be a scene at a rural country station with porter and barrow at the ready as a local train enters- but it is actually Potters Bar as was! N2 0-6-2T **4750** is arriving with the 4.20pm King's Cross to Hatfield on 11th August 1945. This was long before the widening to four tracks and the rebuilding of the station. Local trains such as this calling here and at Hadley Wood to the south posed further limitations on the line's capacity.

This loco was renumbered 9529 by the LNER, then 69529 by BR and was one of the many allocated to Kings Cross. When ousted by dieselisation, it spent a year allocated to Peterborough New England before being withdrawn in September 1962.

Shortly before the train shown in the previous photo, this northbound goods had pounded through the station headed by V2 2-6-2 **4868**. Express passenger, local commuter and goods traffic all had to filter through this bottleneck. Sir Nigel Gresley's 184 V2s were the "engines that won the war" as they could turn their hand to any sort of traffic with ease, particularly fast fitted freight trains such as the one seen here. Indeed the first of the class (now preserved) was named Green Arrow after one such service. This one here became 897 under the 1946 renumbering and then 60897 under BR and was a long term resident of Peterborough New England shed. For its last 21 months it moved to Doncaster from where it was withdrawn in June 1963.

We are now on the four track section north of Potters Bar and this is a real gem, which may well have been published before, but which deserves another outing. This is the super smart Royal Train headed by immaculate "Super Claud" 4-4-0 **8783** on 23rd July 1938. Note the special headcode of all 4 lamps for this train. What a sight it must have been: lined light green loco and teak carriages with white roofs! A local train is disappearing in the distance too.

The 121 locos in this class were constructed between 1900 and 1923 for the Great Eastern Railway (after the formation of the LNER they could be found elsewhere on that system) and had many variants in the batches built. The first of the class was named Claud Hamilton, after a Chairman of the Great Eastern Railway. 8783 was one of the last 1923 batch, designated D16, fitted with a superheater, hence the nickname "Super Claud". This one became 2614 in 1946 and then 62614 under BR and it spent its career based at Kings Lynn (nearest shed to Sandringham, hence its use here) until withdrawn in August 1958.

For his next photograph that day, HCC has moved position to witness A3 Pacific **2555 _Centenary_** on a passenger train. The headcode would suggest that this is a semi-fast. The loco would become 56 in 1946 and then 60056 under BR. It spent time at Kings Cross, Leeds, Doncaster and finally with a ten year spell at Grantham ending in May 1963

CHEAP - 2nd
OFF PEAK
Potters Bar &
South Mimms
to
FINSBURY PARK
3413

A month later HCC was back in the vicinity again, this time by a marvellous bracket of somersault signals. Here is another "Super Claud" 4-4-0 **8787** hauling the 6.55pm King's Cross to Cambridge on 24th August 1938. This was a long-term Cambridge based loco which became 2618 under the 1946 renumbering. It briefly served at Kings Lynn and then March before being withdrawn as 62618 in November 1959.

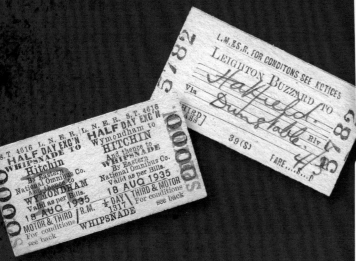

Trains are now due on at least 3 of the 4 lines! Here N2 0-6-2T **4743** is on the 6.10pm from Moorgate St (as it was then called) to Hatfield. This was another of the large stud of these locos that were built for these services and spent its whole life in the area. It became 9522 then 69522 and served at Hornsey, Kings Cross and finally Hitchin from where it was withdrawn in November 1959.

Just to the south of Welwyn **4774**, the fourth member of the handsome V2 2-6-2 class introduced in 1936, heads the 10.20 Scarborough to King's Cross on 19th July 1938. Whereas there were numerous designs of 2-6-2 tank engines in Great Britain, this was the only major class of tender locomotive with this wheel arrangement. This one was only two years old at the time and was in excellent external condition. It became LNER **803** then BR **60803** and spent its life allocated to Peterborough New England and March sheds. It was withdrawn in June 1963, the month steam officially finished working into King's Cross.

A3 Pacific **2751** *Humorist* is on the down Yorkshire Pullman, the 4.45pm Kings Cross to Leeds on 23rd July 1938. To try and improve the ventilation and dispersal of the exhaust (not that any is showing here!), 2751 is fitted with an experimental stubby stove pipe chimney surrounded by small deflectors which rather spoil the graceful appearance of the loco. This was not successful and we shall see the next stage in another photo.

2751 would become 97 and then BR **60097**. It was based at Top Shed (Kings Cross) until July 1950 whereupon it would become a rare loco down south as it migrated to Edinburgh (Haymarket). It was to stay there for the rest of its days, apart from a few months at Carlisle Canal in 1954 and worked over the famous Waverley route. It was withdrawn in August 1963 from Edinburgh St Margarets.

We now move to the south end of Potters Bar Tunnel in the days when there were still only 2 tracks.

What better way to start here than with a powerful picture of the very first built Gresley A4 Pacific, **14 *Silver Link***, rushing south with an express for King's Cross on 31st July 1948. It is here in very early BR days still in LNER blue livery, but when built as 2509 in 1935 it had been silver and grey, hence the name. When it came to the renumbering of the A4s in 1946, they were done according to their names rather than their construction dates, priority being given to those named after the Great and the Good of the LNER. This explains why this one became 14 and not 1. It was also one of the first to go: having served at Top Shed (Kings Cross) and Grantham it was withdrawn as 60014 in December 1962, made redundant by diesels. It is a shame that this historic loco was not one of the ones preserved, priority for the National Collection naturally being given to world record holder ***Mallard***. The story goes that Sir Billy Butlin tried to buy it as one of the locos for display at his holiday camps, but as BR were asking too much for it, he switched his attention to LMS types.

On the same day another A4, **60028 *Walter K Wigham***, is also heading for "The Cross". This one is already in early BR blue livery with "British Railways" in full on the tender. This livery was initially applied by British Railways to the largest locomotives but it did not last long, with the more familiar green taking over. 60028 was another long term resident of Top Shed which was among the first ones to go in December 1962.

What a glorious procession of trains HCC witnessed on that July day in 1948! This is A3 Pacific **44 *Melton*** of Grantham shed on another up express. It is still carrying its LNER identity. It was to spend its BR career based either on the southern part of the ECML or on the former GC system from Marylebone. It was withdrawn in June 1963, the month when steam was officially banned south of Peterborough (though a few steam workings did still manage to work through for a short time!)

We last saw A3 Pacific **60097 *Humorist*** as 2751 north of Potters Bar with the down Yorkshire Pullman, the 4.45 to Leeds back in 1938 when fitted with an experimental exhaust arrangement. Well here it is again ten years later working the same train, again on 31st July 1948. It is now fitted with larger "elephant ear" smoke deflectors, the only one of the class to be so fitted. It kept these even when other members of the class were being fitted with the German type of deflectors which are currently (2020) carried by the preserved Flying Scotsman.

An A3 Pacific on a humble goods train! **60055 *Woolwinder*** is plodding out of Potters Bar tunnel with a southbound goods on 31st July 1948. This was a local A3 shedded at Kings Cross, but it also served at Doncaster. It was an early withdrawal, from Kings Cross in September 1961.

Almost new A2 Pacific **60533 *Happy Knight*** leaves a smoky trail behind as it exits Potters Bar tunnel with a southbound express on 31st July 1948. Not many of these A2s were allocated on the southern section of the ECML, many of them serving north of the border in Scotland. Allocated new to Leeds Copley Hill in April 1948, 60533 subsequently did a lot of shuffling around sheds, serving at Peterborough New England, Grantham, Kings Cross and Doncaster. It was withdrawn in June 1963 from New England.

This is also quite a lowly duty for an A3 Pacific. **89 *Felstead*** is on the 1.50pm All Stations, Peterborough-King's Cross, also on 28th September 1946. Felstead, later 60089, was a local Kings Cross engine until September 1950, then it migrated to Scotland and spent its time based in Edinburgh until withdrawn in October 1963.

Great Northern was reclassified as A1/1 and was easily distinguishable by its unique style of smoke deflectors. However, it was not a particularly successful locomotive and it spent its life working out of sheds at Kings Cross, Peterborough, Grantham and finally Doncaster, from where it was withdrawn in November 1962.

This is a great shot of a unique locomotive (on a down express) and it looks as if there is an enthusiast in the front coach appreciating it! In 1945 Thompson controversially converted the very first Gresley Pacific **4470 *Great Northern*** into the prototype for his new A1 Class. Over the years there has been much speculation as to his motives for choosing that particular A3 to convert. In any case here it is when still new and under the 1946 renumbering scheme it was to become 113, then BR 60113, but here on the 28th September of that year it is still carrying its old A3 number **4470**. Photos of it in service in this state are not common. Thompson retired before any more could be built, so it remained a one-off. Instead A H Peppercorn refined the design and produced his own magnificent A1s, as seen today in the famous new-build Tornado. But that's another story!

B1 4-6-0 **61113** on a down local train formed of some more Quad Arts on 31st July 1948. It is already sporting its BR number and has British railways on the tender, but is still in LNER green. The B1s were Thompsons's most successful design and 410 of them were built, construction continuing into BR days. They were the LNER equivalent of the LMS Black 5s. This one was based at Kings Cross, then moved to Peterborough New England (had a couple of months at Norwich) and spent its last three years at Lincoln, being withdrawn in September 1963.

On 28th September 1946 Sandringham B17 4-6-0 **1631 *Serlby Hall*** is working the 12.55 Cambridge to King's Cross. This class was built mainly for working on the Great Eastern section, but were common on these services. They had also worked on the Great Central section in the 1930s. As 61631 this loco served at Cambridge, March, Stratford and was withdrawn from Ipswich in April 1959.

Here are two views of N2 0-6-2T **4744** on 28th September 1946. Above it is southbound hauling two sets of Quad Art coaches, so called as they consist of four coaches on articulated bogies, meaning that the coaches share wheelsets rather than having their own separate bogies. These were high density commuter coaches and were quite uncomfortable when full. Taller passengers had to interlock knees! If you want to experience these coaches for yourself, a set has been beautifully preserved in the original polished teak along with this very loco on the North Norfolk Railway. Because of its unique heritage, this set usually only comes out on gala days.

Earlier on the same day **4744** was heading north and passed Atlantic 4-4-2 **2868** on an up working. Although HCC has clicked the shutter a fraction late, the photo is nonetheless full of interest, especially as this is the only one of the once 107-strong class to be preserved. 2868 was in the twilight of its career and didn't make it into BR days. A few of the N2s spent their careers in Scotland, but the majority served on Kings Cross suburban services. As 69523, this one moved to Peterborough for its last few months of service in 1962.

We end this section with two views of A4 Pacific 8 **Dwight D. Eisenhower** on a down express on 31st July 1948. It is starting to look a bit scruffy in its LNER blue livery. As 60008 it served on the southern part of the ECML and shared duties between Kings Cross and Grantham sheds. When regular steam workings into Kings Cross finished in June 1963, it was banished to Peterborough New England, but was promptly withdrawn in the following month. However because of its name it was offered to the United States and is preserved at the National Railroad Museum at Green Bay, Wisconsin. In 2012 it temporarily returned to the UK to take part in the Great Gathering of all six surviving A4s in 2013 to celebrate the 75th anniversary of Mallard's record run. It returned to Wisconsin in 2014.

Unusual WCML Workings

The Casserley collection of photographs is a wonderful window onto a world of railways long vanished and even the most ordinary (for the time) of them are of significance to us today. But then, as now, there were always a few workings which were not an everyday occurrence and which deserve special attention. Here therefore is a selection of such workings that HCC managed to photograph.

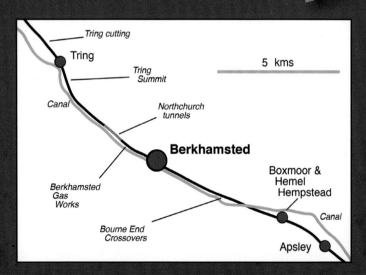

To begin with we have a photograph which complements that on page 74 of the first book. In that we saw a close-up view of some brand new London tube stock for the Northern Line on their delivery run from the Metropolitan Carriage and Wagon Co in Birmingham on 30th March 1939. Here is a more distant view taken from HCC's study at *Ravensbourne* in Berkhamsted of the whole train approaching, hauled by an ex-LNWR 0-8-0.

Also visible in the photo is the bracket of home signals for the down fast and down slow lines with something "pegged" for the down slow. There are also some wagons by the coal drop (seen in a photo in Book One page 98) to the narrow gauge railway to the gasworks in the background that was so well covered in the first book. Also of interest are the green fields all around that are now built-up. The field in the foreground is now occupied by a residential road, South Park Gardens.

Mary Casserley adds: HCC moved to Ravensbourne on 24th March 1939, so this photo was taken less than a week after he moved in.

In absolutely stonkingly good condition, with a finish rarely seen even in the preservation era, BR Standard Britannia Pacific **70004 *William Shakespeare*** is seen from *Ravensbourne* passing through Berkhamsted on 30th March 1951 on its way to London for the Festival of Britain Exhibition on the South Bank. It is brand new and as it is not in steam, it is minus its coupling rods. It is being hauled by Jubilee 4-6-0 **45654 *Hood*** which was a visitor from Millhouses shed and has the early "British Railways" branding on its tender, whereas 70004 has the then new "cycling lion" emblem.

In the 1950s 70004, along with 70014 ***Iron Duke***, was kept in immaculate condition at Stewarts Lane shed for working the "Golden Arrow", somewhat surprisingly, given the large number of Bulleid Pacifics on the Southern Region. It then became a London Midland region loco and often worked through Berkhamsted. Both these locos survived relatively late into the steam era, the Jubilee going in June 1966 and 70004 in December 1967.

Three years later on May 17th 1954 BR Standard Class 5 4-6-0 **73050** in similar condition and also minus some of its rods is being towed south to Willesden shed for exhibition at the International Railway Congress which was held there from 26th-29th May. The exhibition featured examples of the latest motive power on British Railways and HCC attended and photographed the exhibits. Also in the consist, is 0-6-0 diesel shunter 13046 (later D3046, then 08033), also for the exhibition. This then became a Southern Region locomotive until 1968, when it moved to the London Midland Region and then on to Tinsley on the Eastern Region in 1974 until it was withdrawn in 1985.

73050 entered service on the now much lamented Somerset and Dorset Railway where it served in front line service, including on the famous Pines Express, until 1964. On moving away, it survived being withdrawn once and went on to serve until July 1968, almost till the very end of steam that August. It was then secured for preservation and formed the basis for the embryonic Nene Valley Railway at Peterborough where it has been based ever since. It is currently (2021) out of service undergoing overhaul.

Whilst not of particularly good quality, this photo, another taken from *Ravensbourne*, is nonetheless of interest. The Garratt design of steam locomotive was not much in favour on the railways in this country, though many were constructed in the UK for use overseas. The LMS built 33 of them to a 2-6-6-2 design from 1927 onwards and this was the only significant class of them in Britain. They spent their thirty-year career chiefly plodding up and down the Midland Main Line hauling massively long coal trains from the Nottinghamshire coalfields to London, so quite what this one, **7981**, is doing proceeding south, light engine, on the up slow at Berkhamsted on 13th August 1948 is lost in the mists of time. They certainly weren't a common sight on the West Coast Mainline. In the mid-1950s the class was displaced by the BR Standard 9F 2-10-0s and this one was withdrawn in November 1956.

In the first book Richard Casserley showed us some pictures of the famous 1948 Locomotive Exchange Trials, where selected locos in different categories from the former "Big Four" companies were tried out against each other on each other's routes with a view to establishing some standard classes. Here are some more views that HCC took.

On 20th May 1948 A4 Pacific **60034 Lord Faringdon** approaches Berkhamsted with an up express. It has just passed a down train which is receding into the distance and gives the impression that the one hauled by 60034 is longer than it actually was! The signalman has not yet had time to reset the signal.

60034 was the last of this famous class to be constructed and was also one of the last three left in service, being withdrawn on 24th August 1966, just two weeks ahead of the last two (60019 and 60024). After regular main line steam into Kings Cross finished in the summer of 1963, 60034 was one of the lucky ones to enjoy an Indian summer in Scotland, working Glasgow to Aberdeen expresses.

This is one of the most remarkable photographs I have seen of local scenes in the collection. HCC is travelling on the 4.55pm Euston to Tring, presumably on his commute home, and has obviously seen this train further south or waiting to leave Euston and he has had his camera at the ready for when it overtook him. It looks as if it was a close run thing, as he is only a mile or so from his home station of Berkhamsted.

The photo shows ex-Southern Railway Light Pacific **34004 Yeovil** piloting Royal Scot 4-6-0 **6159 The Royal Air Force** on a northbound express. 34004 was another locomotive involved in the 1948 Locomotive Exchanges and it has a long journey ahead of it, as it is heading for testing in Scotland on the Highland main line to Inverness. A very lucky capture indeed on 2nd July 1948.

Also of interest is the coal barge on the Grand Union Canal, a scene that lasted until the 1960s. As a boy I used to enjoy watching these while spotting the trains by the Crystal Palace pub in Berkhamsted.

34004 lost its air smoothed casing when it was rebuilt as a conventional locomotive in February 1958 and then lasted until the very end of Southern Region steam in July 1967. 6159 was a local engine and in the 1950s, as 46159, yo-yoed between being locally based at Camden and being based at Crewe. It was withdrawn from Willesden in December 1962, a date when several members of this famous class were withdrawn.

This one is not all that it seems! On the face of it we see a normal local train headed by a usual 2-6-4 tank engine passing some wonderful wooden-bodied private owner wagons. However **2517** is one of the small class of the 37 Stanier 3-cylinder version (the hundreds of others all had only two cylinders) which were built especially for the London Tilbury and Southend section out of Fenchurch St to improve acceleration on the intense service with frequent stops on that route. Until I saw this photo, I had always thought that these locos spent their whole lives on the Fenchurch St line! According to the note written by RMC on the back of the photo, this loco was allocated to Watford from 1943-1945. I have since also found out that two of the class spent a few months in the Glasgow area in 1951-2. The first of the class, 2500, is preserved at the National Railway Museum. Sadly, not one of the far more common Stanier 2-Cylinder version has been preserved.

The photo was taken from *Ravensbourne* on the beautiful sunny morning of 8th July 1944. You wouldn't think there was a war on, would you?

Another one from the 1948 Locomotive Exchange trials. The evening sunlight is bouncing off the air-smoothed casing (the official term for the SR Pacifics, not streamlining!) of Merchant Navy **35017 Belgian Marine** as it heads the 12.55 Carlisle-Euston out of Northchurch tunnel on a glorious 14th May 1948. As Richard Casserley explained in the first volume, it is equipped with a Stanier LMS tender which has a scoop so it can pick up water from troughs en route. The tenders of SR locos were not so equipped. In any case, water troughs would not have worked with the spreading third rail electrification!

All 30 of this class (though at the date of this photograph the final ten had yet to be built) subsequently had the casing removed and were rebuilt as conventional locomotives during the second half of the 1950s. Thanks to being sold to Dai Woodham's scrapyard in Barry, South Wales, no fewer than eleven of the class have survived into preservation, though this is not one of them. Not all have yet been restored, but the team in charge of 35011 are intending to "un-rebuild" it, so hopefully before too long we will see this shape take to the rails again.

It would never happen today! We now jump forward to the modern era, but before the time of the dreaded Rail Replacement Bus Service! In the early years of electrification, when the power had to be switched off for maintenance work at weekends, diesels would be drafted in to haul the electric passenger trains through the dead section and that is what is happening here on Sunday 5th May 1974. This is something that I also photographed, though not on this same occasion. Class 47 no **47208**, recently renumbered from D1858 and still in two-tone green livery, is hauling a Class 310 electric unit on a local service on the down fast. The Class 310 (formerly AM10) 4-car Electric Multiple Units were a stylish design, particularly with the original wrap-round front windows. They were built for the electrification of the line and were based on the Mk2 coach body. The motor coach was one of the middle coaches and initially there was no corridor connection through the end of the coach where some of the motor equipment was situated, thus making them in effect 2+2-car units. They were later modified with a connection right through. For the enthusiast there was the added bonus that by kneeling up on the front seats you could have a view forward behind the driver. They were built mainly for passenger and suburban

services south of Birmingham and revolutionised travel on the line, bringing a regular interval service with frequent trains throughout the day, whereas before electrification the service had been very sparse indeed, as mentioned earlier.

47208 was at the time based at Crewe, but later that same month it would migrate to Scotland. Sadly it would be involved in a fatal accident at Invergowrie on 22nd October 1979 when it ran into the back of a stationary local train. The damage to the loco was so severe that it was written off.

In the background of the photo we can see that the goods yard has closed and all the track has been lifted, but it is yet to become the inevitable car park.

When I first saw this photograph it had me puzzled! What could it be? It looks like a GWR 0-6-0 Pannier tank with condensing apparatus, yet with a tender and that's exactly what it is-sort of. As part of the war effort for the Second World War, the War Department commandeered locomotives for service abroad (as well as ordering the construction of new locomotives for this role). From the GWR they took just over a hundred of the veteran Dean Goods 0-6-0s, some of which had also served abroad in the First World War! Of these tender locomotives, just ten had pannier tanks with condensing apparatus added to them and with the fact that it was taken in the middle of the war, this photograph is a very rare one indeed!

WD177 is seen from HCC's *Ravensbourne* home scuttling south on the up main in October 1942. He was all the more lucky to see it as, according to his diary, for most of that month his work meant that he and the family were based in Derby.

NB The grass roller which can be seen by the summer house in the lower left-hand corner of the picture is still in the garden of the Casserley family home.

As part of the development work for the HST, AL6 (Class 86) **E3173** was fitted with an experimental nose to test performance and turbulence when passing other trains in tunnels. The AL6s had earlier caused problems by the weight of their unsprung axle hung traction motors pounding and damaging the track. So in 1969 E3173 had been fitted with flexicoil springs to try and solve the problem (subsequently adopted for the class). This gave the loco the nickname "Zebedee", named after the character with a spring in "The Magic Roundabout" and it was this loco that was selected for the high speed tests. Here are two views of it passing Berkhamsted in May 1971. The nose closely resembles that eventually carried by the prototype HST.

E3173 became 86204 and was named *City of Carlisle* and was withdrawn in August 1998 and scrapped at Immingham five years later.

The New Order

HCC did not like diesels. Indeed whenever he could, he would avoid travelling behind one and would even change trains and wait for steam if a diesel came onto his train! Fortunately, and perhaps surprisingly given this attitude, he did nonetheless turn his camera towards the new interlopers and there are quite a few diesel photos in the collection.

The writing was on the wall for his beloved LMS steam locomotives with the announcement of general dieselisation and the electrification of the West Coast Main Line under the 1955 Modernisation Plan. Since the late 1940s and early 1950s there had been the two LMS and three SR main line diesel prototypes, but these were viewed as curiosities rather than any real threat. That was to change from 1959 onwards on the WCML when the English Electric Type 4s (later to be Class 40) and Derby Sulzer Type 2s (later to be Class 24, the slightly more powerful Class 25 version didn't come until a few years later) came onto the scene in large numbers, along with some English Electric Type 1s (later Class 20), quickly displacing steam, particularly on passenger workings. The diesels themselves were banished when the electrification came on stream in 1966 (1967 to Birmingham) and it has been easy to question with hindsight why they had to go to the trouble of building expensive diesels and training up crews for such a relatively short time instead of keeping steam going right up to electrification. However, the bigger picture needs to be considered and one factor was that maintaining a steam fleet was labour intensive, physically hard and dirty work with long hours and in the bright new post-war world it was getting harder to recruit manpower when there were plenty of more attractive new jobs on offer elsewhere.

The English Electric Type 4s in particular, though they later did some admirable freight and secondary passenger work, were not really suited to everyday top link duties as they were rather heavy and under-powered for the job, so there was little improvement in express passenger timings over steam, especially with all the speed restrictions that had to be imposed while electrification work was going on. However, the diesels did not need servicing as often as steam, so could be worked more intensively and of course they were far more comfortable for the crew. It wasn't until the electrics came along that there was a quantum leap in the service though.

It was nonetheless a fascinating, if all too short, period of transition for the enthusiast, so let's now look at some Casserley diesel and electric photos, starting with the prototypes.

Previous page: One of the famous LMS twins (though this one was completed by BR) Co-Co **10001** enters past the shed at Watford Jct on 17th January 1959 on the Saturdays-only 12.40 Bletchley to Euston. Along with the three Southern Railway prototypes (see next picture) they worked various passenger and goods services including the prestigious Royal Scot. However by this date the English Electric Type 4s were about to enter service and the prototypes were given more and more humble duties such as this local. No 10000 didn't work again after December 1962 and was stored at Derby works, but 10001 soldiered on until March 1966 and during this time I remember seeing it sitting on a weekend engineering train south of Berkhamsted. After withdrawal it spent nearly two years stored at the back of the new Willesden Diesel and Electric depot, but sadly this was before any thought was given to preserving diesels and it was cut up nearby in Acton at the beginning of 1968. Strangely 10000, although long withdrawn, actually survived 10001 by a month or so before being cut up itself.

On shed is a BR Standard 4MT 2-6-4T. These were allocated new to the area in the mid-1950s, but were soon to be swapped for Southern Region, Brighton-built, Fairburn versions of the type.

Prototype 1 Co-Co 1 **10203** enters Watford Jct with the 4.15 to Bletchley on 23rd July 1955. The three SR diesels 10201-3 had an obvious Bulleid Southern Railway influence in their design, but they didn't enter service until a few years after Nationalisation, in 1950, 1951 and 1954 respectively. This one was therefore only just over a year old when this photo was taken and it had also only been transferred from the Southern Region just three weeks earlier. These locos and the LMS twins all spent time on both the Southern and London Midland Region being evaluated in the 1950s. 10203 was more powerful than the other two of its class and although of very different appearance, was a direct ancestor of the English Electric Type 4s which first appeared in 1958. It is in the then standard livery for the main line diesels of black with silver lining.

Along with 10000, 10201-3 were stored at Derby Works from the end of 1962 and lingered on until they were finally cut up in early 1968.

3rd-SINGLE SINGLE-3rd
Watford Junc
Watford Junc   Watford Junc
No3   (No3
Tring   Tring
TRING
FARE   2/3H (M
2/3 H   For conditions see over

A photo which epitomises the transition from steam to diesel! English Electric Type 4 **D292** is picking up water from Bushey troughs whilst heading a Euston to Manchester express on 15th October 1960. D292 has been fitted with a scoop so that it can pick up water to replenish its steam heating boiler. Being of the steam era, the coaching stock of the time was equipped only for steam heating, so diesels for passenger services in the winter months had to be fitted with boilers to provide the steam. These could be a real headache at times, as some were very unreliable. On the WCML new coaching stock was gradually introduced with electric train heating to go with the electric locomotives, but even after electrification some trains had to include specially converted boiler vans for a short while, as there was still so much steam-heated coaching stock around. (bottom left).

D292 became 40092 under the TOPS renumbering of the 1970s. It lasted until November 1982 and for the last eight years of its working life it was an Eastern Region locomotive. After withdrawal it was briefly used for re-railing and breakdown exercises in Temple Mills yard. It ended up at Swindon Works and lingered there before being cut up a couple of years or so later.

Coach converted into boiler van M44418M in a train hauled by an electric locomotive (AL4 E3044) at Manchester Piccadilly on 29th April 1961.

There's a very interesting assortment of vehicles in this southbound stock working headed by EE Type 4 **D342**. It has just left Northchurch tunnel on the up slow. It is the 14th September 1963 and the electrification infrastructure is taking shape. At this stage there are as yet no wires and the crosses show that the new signals are not yet operational.

D342 was one of a batch of twenty (D325-D344) that were built with split headcode boxes. It became Class 40 40142 and spent the last six years of its working career based in Scotland, at Haymarket (Edinburgh) depot. It was withdrawn in April 1980 following collision damage. It was cut up at Crewe Works in 1983.

A powerful photo of **D232** on the down Ulster Express, note the headboard, on a sunny evening on 9th August 1963 as it passes through Berkhamsted, the north end of the goods yard is visible on the left. The loco is in superb condition with gleaming bodyside and the small yellow warning panel, red buffer beam and the only slightly tarnished silver buffers really stand out in the evening sun. The gantries for the forthcoming electrification are starting to appear at this date.

As the name implies, The Ulster Express served Northern Ireland, via the ferry link at Heysham to Belfast. It left Euston at 6.10pm. The service ended in 1975 when the Heysham-Belfast ferry was withdrawn.

Apart from D226 whose allocated name Media was never carried, D210-D235 were named after ships of Cunard, Elder Dempster Lines and Canadian Pacific Steamships whose homeport was

Liverpool, one of the places these locos regularly served. D232 was named Empress of Canada, a ship of the latter company and later became Class 40 40032. It was always a London Midland Region locomotive and was withdrawn from Longsight (Manchester) on 1st February 1981. It was cut up at Swindon Works in 1983.

Another transition shot showing **D228** on an express approaching Berkhamsted station on the up fast on 12ᵗʰ October 1963. The semaphore signals are still in operation for the time being, including the marvellous bracket signal on the down slow, but the frame for the electric replacement is in place. In the background is the new goods unloading bay in the goods yard. There is an interesting gantry above the locomotive: it has no vertical support on the right-hand side. This was to accommodate the track to the sidings in the yard, though this was to close before too long. The gantry is still like this to this day!

D228 was named after a Cunard ship *Samaria* and it became Class 40 40028. Apart from a couple of months based at Healey Mills, Wakefield, it was always a London Midland Region locomotive. It was withdrawn from Longsight (Manchester) on 19ᵗʰ October 1984 and cut up at Swindon Works a year or so later.

For a brief period from 1960 until early 1962, the original 10 "Peak" Class diesels numbered D1-D10 (later Class 44) were allocated to the West Coast mainline to help work expresses until the full complement of English Electric Type 4s was delivered. They thus had a brief moment in the limelight before being banished to Toton for the rest of their twenty year or so working lives to haul freight trains around the Midlands. They were not quite as powerful as the following series of the class. They were called "Peaks" as they were named after English and Welsh mountains. The name persisted for the rest of the 193 strong class (later classes 45 and 46), although it was only these ten that were so named.

Here we see the class leader itself, **D1** *Scafell Pike*, on an up express about to pass through Berkhamsted on the up fast on 24ᵗʰ June 1961. Note the tall signals for improved sighting on the long curve to the north of the station. The goods unloading bay in the background must have been a late and short lived addition, as it does not feature in earlier photos. It obscures a view of the Casserley home *Ravensbourne*!

The Derby Sulzer Type 2s (later Class 24) began to appear on local passenger services, sharing workings with Fairburn 2-6-4Ts. I can remember as a boy when being taken to London for a day out always hoping it would be steam and not a dreaded "D50er"! Here we see **D5032** approaching Berkhamsted with an up local on 14th October 1961. It has not yet been fitted with a yellow warning panel. This loco is of interest as it is still with us today. When withdrawn as 24032 from Crewe in 1976, it was sold to T J Thomson Ltd of Stockton for scrap and it moved there under its own power. However, almost immediately the North Yorkshire Moors Railway managed to secure the long term loan of

the loco and it has remained based there ever since, named *Helen Turner* after the daughter of one of the scrap dealer's directors. It is currently out of service undergoing overhaul.

The coaches are the standard LMS non-corridor type. The compartments were decorated with prints of travel in bygone days and some of these prints can now be seen on display in various museums eg in that at the Buckinghamshire Railway Centre at Quainton Road.

Also of interest in this photo to residents of Berkhamsted are the newly constructed houses of South Park Gardens.

Here we see **D5073** and **D5080** heading a down local departing from Berkhamsted on 19th September 1964 with a train formed of LMS corridor coaches. The electrification is now complete here and the testing of electric locomotives commenced that same month. As 24073 and 24080 both these locomotives were withdrawn from Crewe after being in store and were cut up at Doncaster Works in 1978.

From D5113 onwards the Sulzer Type 2s, later Class 24, were fitted with headcode boxes as were all the later, slightly more powerful Class 25s. The first twenty of this batch D5113 to D5132 were allocated to the far north lines of Scotland, but the next ones D5133 to D5146 were allocated to the WCML. Here we see the first of these, **D5133**, entering Berkhamsted with an up local formed of LMS corridor coaches on 24th June 1961. It has no yellow waring panel as yet, giving it a rather drab appearance. It is passing its tall home signal and the magnificent bracket signal on the down slow which still had a few a few years to go before being swept away by the electrification of the line.

D5133 survived to be one of the last Class 24s in traffic and on 14th January 1978 24133, which it had become by then, worked the Merseyside Express from St Pancras to Liverpool Lime Street, via circuitous routes, out via Shrewsbury and back via Stoke on Trent. It was double-heading with 24082 and was one of the farewell tours to the class and billed as the last Class 24-worked passenger train from London. I was on board and I remember it as one of those dreary winter days when it hardly got light all day, which made photography difficult and it certainly did not help the mood of the occasion!

The English Electric Type 1s (later Class 20) were the first of the diesels ordered under the 1955 Modernisation Plan to appear, in 1957, and the first ones were allocated to the London area. They turned out to be one of the most successful of the early designs with some examples still working in service past their 60th birthday! On our section of the WCML they were used to haul pick-up and other goods traffic and even the occasional local passenger train (though they were not fitted with train heating equipment, so hopefully just in the summer months!).

Here, from over the fence of HCC's garden, we see the very first of the class, **D8000**, shunting in Berkhamsted yard on a murky 22nd February 1967. It is already ten years old and in splendid external condition, so presumably has had a recent works visit, though interestingly it has reappeared in original green livery (though with yellow warning panel): Rail Blue was starting to be introduced at this time.

The class were withdrawn over a considerable length of time and this historic locomotive, now numbered 20050, was withdrawn as long ago as 1980, some 40 years before the last survivors! It was passed to the National Railway Museum but it was another five years before it was restored at Doncaster Works for display at the museum in York.

In the background of the photo, just behind the locomotive, is part of the mail pick up apparatus which featured in the first book.

Later during the shunt the loco has attached diesel brake tender 984028. It was found that some diesels lacked the brake force of steam locos when hauling unfitted goods trains (i.e. wagons with no brakes, of which thousands still existed at the time) and the solution was to build these vehicles to add braking power to the trains.

Mary Casserley adds: This was the day I was born!

Here's quite a rarity: the BRCW Type 2s, later Class 26, are mostly associated with Scotland, but when they were introduced in 1959, the first twenty of the class spent their first 15 months or so allocated to Hornsey for working local passenger and freight in the Kings Cross district. They migrated north in the spring of 1960. So in the short period they were down south, here we see **D5305** on an eastbound goods consisting of mineral wagons at Harpenden East on the line from Luton Bute Street (and beyond to Dunstable and Leighton Buzzard) to Hatfield.

Note the somersault signal. The date is 5th September 1959. The line here was to close to passengers in April 1965.

D5305 had a 34 year career and as 26005 it was withdrawn from Edinburgh Haymarket depot in October 1993. In its latter years it was one of a handful of the class (26001-26007) that were fitted with slow speed control for working Merry Go Round coal trains (which loaded and unloaded on the move at very low speed-1mph or less).

And so to the electric era. The electrification of the West Coast Main Line to Crewe and Manchester was opened in stages extending southwards (planners of HS2 please take note!) from 1959 to 1966, and 1967 via Birmingham. As each section was energised, extensive testing took place. The original 100 electric locomotives were built by five different builders, all to the same basic external design, and classified AL1 (25 locos), AL2 (10 locos), AL3 (15 locos), AL4 10 locos) and AL5 (40 locos) and numbered E3001-E3100. They were equipped with different electrical gear internally and the different designs of ventilation grilles, different on each side of the bodyside, distinguished each class. They later became BR Classes 81-85.

Here we see two views of AL1 locomotive **E3003** (later 81002) stabled at Tring between test train duties on 16th July 1965, showing the detail differences of grilles and windows on each side. If you are wondering why this loco became 81002 and not 81003, it is because E3002 was withdrawn with fire damage before renumbering took place. Sadly two other AL1s and two AL2s also suffered fire or accident damage and were also never renumbered. Five of the original electrics have been preserved, one of each type, and this happens to be the AL1 example, preserved at Barrow Hill.

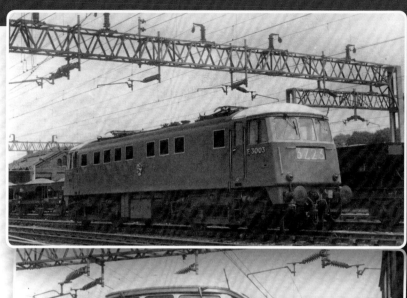

Also at Tring on that July day in 1965 we see AL2 **E3048** passing on a down test train. The headcode appears to be 7Z23: the first figure must be incorrect as that means an express freight train without continuous brake! The coaching stock appears to consist of redundant non-corridor coaches from elsewhere, as the first one is numbered SC43325 (Scottish Region).

E3048 became Class 82 82002 and lasted in service until August 1983. It was cut up a year or so later at Vic Berry's of Leicester.

HCC had taken hundreds of photos of steam locos from his home and garden in Berkhamsted over the years, but now he had to resort to an electric! On New Year's Day 1966 AL5 **E3073** is passing on an up goods. Full electric services from Euston were to start from the following April, but before that, electric locomotives were first used on freight trains to and from Wembley yard.

The AL5s were built by BR themselves in their Doncaster workshops. How ironic that these locos (and forty of the later Class AL6) for the WCML were built at the bastion of the former rival ECML route! The Class 85s (and Class 81s), as they became, were the more successful of the five early designs and E3073, as 85018, lasted in service until October 1991.

HCC obviously kept his lineside pass into the modern era! It is 18th May 1966 and just one month after full electric services were inaugurated from Euston, although it would be 6th March of the following year before the Birmingham line became electric.

Here we see a good example of how initially the line was in some respects really just an electrified steam railway! A modern locomotive AL2 **E3051** is hauling a rake of 16 ton mineral wagons northbound through Platform 2 at Berkhamsted. It was in the attractive bright new livery of electric blue with small yellow warning panel and white cab windows and roof. It would later become 82005 and end its days hauling empty stock workings between Euston and Wembley. In so doing, along with 82008, it outlived the other members of the class by some 4 years, being finally withdrawn in October 1987.

HCC says in his diary that this week was the 50th anniversary of his first recorded solo rail journey: a suitable note to end this section on!

GLOSSARY

HCC - Henry Cyril Casserley
RMC - Richard Michael Casserley

SLS - Stephenson Locomotive Society
RCTS - The Rail Correspondence and
Travel Society

GC - Great Central
GWR - Great Western Railway
MML - Midland Main Line
WCML - West Coast Main Line
ECML - East Coast Main Line

DMU - Diesel Multiple Unit
EMU - Electric Multiple Unit
HST - High Speed Train
TPO - Travelling Post Office

Pacific - steam loco with a 4-6-2 wheel arrangement

Prairie - steam loco with a 2-6-2 wheel arrangement

Pannier Tank: - steam loco that carries water in tanks on either side of the

boiler only, peculiar to the GWR

Autocoach/auto-trailer - coach that has driving controls at one end, so that

the locomotive doesn't have to run round at the end of each journey, provided
it has been equipped for such working.

Pick-up goods train - train that visits local stations attaching and detaching
wagons.

Diesel Locomotives Power Classifications according to horsepower
Type 1 1,000hp or less
Type 2 1,001-1499hp
Type 3 1500-1999hp
Type 4 2,000-2,999hp
Type 5 3,000hp or more

In compiling these captions, I have used my own knowledge and various books,
periodicals and websites. Too many to mention in full, but here are some of the
main ones:
BR Steam Locomotives 1948-1968 by Hugh Longworth
The Allocation History of BR Diesels and Electrics by Roger Harris
Websites: Six Bells Junction website, websites of various Loco Groups, Wikipedia.